W9-CMM-770

WORKFORCE: BUILDING SUCCESS

TEACHER'S GUIDE

Project Consultant

Harriet Diamond
Diamond Associates
Westfield, NJ

Series Reviewers

Nancy Arnold
Metropolitan Adult
Education Program
San Jose, CA

Lou Winn Burns
Booker High School
Sarasota, FL

Jane Westbrook
Weatherford ISD
Community Services
Weatherford, TX

Ronald D. Froman
National Training &
Development Specialists
Winter Springs, FL

Dr. Randy Whitfield
North Carolina Community
College System
Raleigh, NC

Ann Jackson
Orange County
Public Schools
Orlando, FL

STECK-VAUGHN
C O M P A N Y
ELEMENTARY • SECONDARY • ADULT • LIBRARY

Acknowledgments

Steck-Vaughn Company
Executive Editor: Ellen Northcutt
Supervising Editor: Tim Collins
Senior Editor: Julie Higgins
Assistant Art Director: Richard Balsam
Design Manager: Danielle Szabo

Proof Positive/Farrowlyne Associates, Inc.
Program Editorial, Development, Design, and Production

ISBN 0-8172-6523-6

4 5 6 7 8 9 DBH 01 00

Contents

About SCANS, the Workforce, and Steck-Vaughn's *Workforce: Building Success*

SCANS and the Workforce

The Secretary's Commission on Achieving Necessary Skills (SCANS) was established by the U.S. Department of Labor in 1990. Its mission was to study the demands of workplace environments and determine whether people entering the workforce are capable of meeting those demands. The commission identified skills for employment, suggested ways for assessing proficiency, and devised strategies to implement the identified skills. This commission's first report, entitled *What Work Requires of Schools—SCANS Report for America 2000,* was published in June, 1991. The report is designed for use by educators (curriculum developers, job counselors, training directors, teachers) to prepare the modern workforce for the workplace with viable, up-to-date skills.

The report identified two types of skills: Competencies and Foundations. There are five SCANS Competencies: (1) Resources; (2) Interpersonal; (3) Information; (4) Systems; and (5) Technology. There are three parts contained in SCANS Foundations: (1) Basic Skills (including reading, writing, arithmetic, mathematics, listening, and speaking); (2) Thinking Skills (including creative thinking, decision making, problem solving, seeing things in the mind's eye, knowing how to learn, and reasoning); and (3) Personal Qualities (including responsibility, self-esteem, sociability, self-management, and integrity/honesty).

Steck-Vaughn's *Workforce: Building Success*

Each book of *Workforce: Building Success* incorporates SCANS Competencies and Foundation skills. The books are designed to ensure comprehension and develop skills to prepare students for the workplace. For example, *Problem Solving* presents a problem-solving process based on the SCANS Foundations Thinking Skill, Problem Solving. The *Writing* book focuses on Basic Skills (reading and writing) and Competencies (information, systems, and technology) to prepare the student for the writing skills necessary to get a job and to write well on the job.

On pages 4 and 5, you will find a SCANS Correlation Chart presenting the Competencies and Thinking Skills listed by book in the *Workforce: Building Success* series. Also provided are sample occupations, which appear in the case studies in the books, and a description of the Competencies.

About the Student Books and the Teacher's Guide

The Student Books

The *Workforce: Building Success* series is designed to help students improve key job skills whether they are already working or are preparing to find a job. The *Communication* book covers listening effectively, giving and receiving feedback, and effective telephone communication. *Time Management* focuses on skills necessary to manage, delegate, and plan job tasks. *Personal Development* focuses on career development, performance appraisals, and the management of stress. *Customer Service* presents the concepts of internal and external customers, the worker's responsibilities to each type of customer, and the use of technology to meet work goals. In the first five lessons of *Problem Solving*, students are guided through a process of steps to build confidence for solving problems; the remaining lessons present ways to apply those problem-solving steps to workplace challenges. The *Writing* book focuses on skills necessary for writing to get a job and writing on the job.

Each book contains two **Skills Inventories.** At the beginning of each book, the **Check What You Know** establishes students' "starting point" for the skills presented in the book. A Preview Chart shows students what skills they will improve as they proceed with the book. To follow up, **Check What You've Learned** tests students' mastery of the material. A Review Chart follows the Check What You've Learned. Students may compare their Review Chart with their Preview Chart to see how much they have improved their skills.

The **Lesson Opener** page in each unit contains the following elements: prereading questions, a purpose statement, and a photo. Teachers are encouraged to use these elements to stimulate class discussion. Prereading questions help set a purpose for reading. The purpose statement and photo are designed to capture student interest and engage them with the material. **Case Studies** appear in every lesson to highlight real-life workplace situations and to illustrate key points of the lesson content. Case Studies often include a photo. A variety of industries is represented, including: health care, business and retail, construction, service, manufacturing, and food service. The Case Studies represent entry-level careers which are within students' reach. Interaction as part of a team, working with technology, and managing time are just some of the topics presented within these real-life workplace scenarios.

Four types of exercises are featured. The questions in **Comprehension Check** will help students check their understanding of the lesson's content. **Making Connections** offers case studies that call for students to analyze and propose solutions for the scenarios presented, which will help them develop their critical thinking skills. The interactive activity, which is called **Try It Out, Act It Out,** or **Talk It Out,** allows students to explore one aspect of the lesson's content in greater depth through an in-class activity or by talking to workers, supervisors, and managers in their community. These activities help students realize the relevance of the text's content to the workplace as they talk with people who use the skills covered in the lesson. The **Think and Apply** page is ideal for students to use for self-assessment and will help them plan how to develop their skills beyond the classroom.

An **Answer Key** is provided for answers to **Comprehension Check** and **Making Connections** exercises. An end-of-book **Glossary** defines terms that appear in dark print in the text.

The *Writing* book begins with a **Self-Inventory of Writing Skills,** which assesses students' writing skills. Lessons include models of forms, letters, and other business documents commonly found in the workplace. Lessons are followed by three types of exercises—**Vocabulary Check, Comprehension Check,** and **Apply the Skill.**

In most lessons, students practice creating a business document. At the end of the book is a Handbook, which explains rules of the English language. The last part of the Handbook, the Writing Process, presents simplified steps and practice in how to write.

The Teacher's Guide
The *Teacher's Guide* is designed to enhance the content, activities, and learning opportunities in the student books. The *Teacher's Guide* contains a variety of strategies requiring minimal or no preparation time. **About the Book** presents an overview of the philosophy and goals of each book. About the Book contains the following elements: **Student Goals:** a list of skills and knowledge to be attained in class; **SCANS Foundation Skills:** a list of workplace competencies, Basic Skills, and Thinking Skills; and **Reading Skills:** a correlation between the **Comprehension Check** student pages and key TABE (Tests of Adult Basic Education) reading skills.

Following About the Book are teaching strategies for each lesson. The *Teacher's Guide* offers several features and strategies for each lesson of each book: **Objectives:** a list of student goals for the lesson; **Vocabulary:** words that appear in dark type in the lesson and are defined in the **Glossary; Getting Started—Motivational Activity:** a creative way to begin study of the lesson; it highlights the relevance of the text to students' lives; **Introducing the Lesson—Using the Unit Opener:** suggestions for using the photo opener, photo caption, and prereading questions; **Follow-Up—Extension Activity:** ideas for ways to enhance the content of the lesson; **Portfolio Activity:** allows students to respond to the content through written self-expression.

At the end of the *Teacher's Guide* are six **Certificates of Completion,** one for each book in the series, which can be duplicated and given to students upon their completion of the books.

Correlation of SCANS to *Workforce: Building Success*

Book	Thinking Skills	Workplace Competencies	Sample Occupations	Examples of Competencies
Communication	• Knowing How to Learn	• Interpersonal • Information	• apprentice photographer • apprentice plumber • home health aide • product assembler	• **Interpersonal:** Participates and communicates as a member of a team • **Information:** Interprets and communicates information
Time Management	• Decision Making • Problem Solving	• Resources • Information • Interpersonal	• dental assistant • court reporter • firefighter • teacher's aide	• **Resources:** Allocates time • **Information:** Organizes and maintains information Interprets and communicates information • **Interpersonal:** Participates as a member of a team
Personal Development	• Decision Making • Knowing How to Learn	• Interpersonal • Systems	• apprentice carpenter • commercial collector • emergency dispatcher • receptionist	• **Interpersonal:** Participates as a member of a team Serves clients/customers Exercises leadership Negotiates to arrive at a decision • **Systems:** Monitors and corrects performance

Book	Thinking Skills	Workplace Competencies	Sample Occupations	Examples of Competencies
Customer Service	• Decision Making • Problem Solving • Knowing How to Learn	• Information • Interpersonal • Technology	• emergency medical technician • reservations clerk • respiratory care technician • ticket agent	• **Information:** Interprets and communicates information Uses computer to process information • **Interpersonal:** Participates as a member of a team Serves clients/customers Negotiates to arrive at a decision • **Technology:** Applies technology to a task
Problem Solving	• Decision Making • Problem Solving	• Interpersonal • Information • Resources • Systems • Technology	• forklift operator • licensed practical nurse • special events coordinator • X-ray technician	• **Interpersonal:** Participates as a member of a team Exercises leadership Negotiates to arrive at a decision • **Information:** Acquires and evaluates information • **Resources:** Allocates material resources Allocates human resources • **Systems:** Improves and designs systems • **Technology:** Applies technology to a task
Writing	• Decision Making	• Information • Systems • Technology	• dental assistant • receptionist • lab technician	• **Information:** Acquires and evaluates information Organizes information Interprets information • **Systems:** Understands systems • **Technology:** Applies technology to a task

* The Basic Skills of reading, writing, listening, and speaking are integrated throughout the *Workforce: Building Success* series.

Communication

Communication

About the Book
Business leaders cite communication as one of the most important skills needed to succeed in the workplace. Today's work teams and service-oriented industries demand excellent speaking and listening skills of workers at all levels. By improving their speaking and listening skills, learners will certainly see immediate benefits.

This book covers such topics as communication styles; how culture influences style; listening skills; how to handle difficult situations; giving and receiving criticism; resolving problems; and participating effectively as a member of a work team.

Student Goals
- Understand their personal communication style
- Appreciate the diversity of communication styles and develop skills to work with that diversity
- Develop interpersonal skills and communication skills to enable participation in work teams
- Enhance self-confidence in speaking and listening skills

SCANS Foundation Skills

Workplace Competencies: Interpersonal, Information

Basic Skills: Reading, Listening

Thinking Skill: Knowing How to Learn

Reading Skills: Identifying Details, Making Inferences, Identifying Relevant Details

Lesson 1: Listening Effectively (Pages 4–11)

Objectives
Students will learn:
- how to receive, interpret, and respond to verbal messages and other cues.
- how and when to ask questions to acquire and interpret information.

Vocabulary
verbal cues, nonverbal cues, summarize

Getting Started—Motivational Activity
Purpose: to demonstrate that effective listening is necessary for complete communication.
1. Ask each student to write brief directions of how to get to a certain location or how to do something.
2. Ask a volunteer to read his or her directions to the group. Then ask someone to restate what was said. Have the class listen and decide whether the second student repeated accurately.
3. Then, have that student read his or her directions. Continue until everyone both reads and repeats.

Introducing the Lesson—Using the Unit Opener
Use the photo, the photo caption, and the questions on page 4 to get students to talk about the lesson topic. Launch a discussion about situations when students needed to listen to accomplish a task or project at school or work. Ask questions such as:
- What do you do when you need to listen?
- Did you ask questions when you were unsure of something?
- Did anyone summarize what had been said? If *yes*, how was that helpful? If *no*, was there disagreement as to what had been said?

Follow Up—Extension Activity
Ask learners why people sometimes don't listen. Is the speaker doing something the listener doesn't like? Is the listener bored? Then explain that there are listening barriers—attitudes or behaviors on the part of the speaker and/or listener that block communication. Brainstorm a class list of listening barriers, such as not understanding words or phrases, having an angry tone of voice, or not having time to listen.

Portfolio Activity
Have students write a journal entry about a time they were successful listeners.

Communication

Lesson 2: Asking the Right Questions (Pages 12–19)

Objectives
Students will learn:
- how to get information to perform job tasks.
- how to avoid misunderstandings.
- how to ask for clarification.

Vocabulary
communication barriers, slang, jargon

Getting Started—Motivational Activity
Purpose: to demonstrate that obtaining information to perform job tasks is part of effective communication.
1. Ask students to imagine that they have been given an assignment for this class or at work. The assignment is handed over in a file folder without any instructions.
2. Have students write a list of three questions they think of upon receiving the imaginary folder.
3. Have students share their list of questions with the class. Discuss what should be included in giving an assignment.

Introducing the Lesson—Using the Unit Opener
Use the photo, the photo caption, and the questions on page 12 to get students to talk about the lesson topic. Begin a discussion about situations when students need information to perform a task at school or work. Ask questions such as:
- What do you do when you don't understand someone?
- How do you ask for more explanation?
- What do you do if you don't understand a word?

Follow Up—Extension Activity
Ask students why misunderstandings occur. Are listeners too shy to ask questions? Is the speaker talking too quickly or using jargon? Explain that workers are responsible for getting the information they need to do their work. Brainstorm a class list of reasons why misunderstandings occur at home, school, or work. What could have prevented the misunderstandings?

Portfolio Activity
Have students write a list of questions they might want to ask on their first day on the job.

Lesson 3: Giving Clear Directions; Getting Clear Directions (Pages 20–27)

Objectives
Students will learn:
- how to use visual aids to communicate information.
- how to be an active listener.
- how to paraphrase instructions.

Vocabulary
visual aids, point of view, interpret, paraphrasing

Getting Started—Motivational Activity
Purpose: to demonstrate that people rely on information from each other in order to work on common tasks.
1. Ask students to work with a partner.
2. One student writes about how to do something such as baking bread. The student explains the directions as he or she writes them. The other student asks questions for clarification.
3. Students can switch roles and repeat the activity. Discuss which were the most commonly asked questions.

Introducing the Lesson—Using the Unit Opener
Use the photo, the photo caption, and the questions on page 20 to get students to talk about the lesson topic. Discuss situations at work or school when it is important to get directions. Ask questions such as:
- When you are required to use machinery or other equipment, why is it important to get directions first?
- Have you ever been given directions that were incorrect? What happened?
- When you give directions, how do you show someone what you mean?
- How can you know if the listener understood your directions?

Follow Up—Extension Activity
Have students work in groups of three. Divide different sections of a newspaper and distribute them to students. Have one student in each group volunteer to read aloud a short article in the paper. The two other students repeat or paraphrase the content of the article. Have students switch roles and repeat the activity.

Portfolio Activity
Have students write a journal entry about a time they were given unclear directions by a store employee or service person.

Communication

Lesson 4: Giving a Clear Message (Pages 28–35)

Objectives
Students will learn:
- how to choose words carefully.
- how to pay attention to body language.

Vocabulary
vocabulary, nonverbal messages

Getting Started—Motivational Activity
Purpose: to demonstrate that words and actions affect the meaning of messages.
1. Give students an example of a positive and a negative message.
2. Ask students to make some facial expressions and other gestures for each type of message.
3. Discuss what would happen if the positive gestures and expressions were paired with negative messages. What would happen if negative gestures and expressions were paired with positive messages? Lead them to conclude that it is important for body language to match the verbal message.

Introducing the Lesson—Using the Unit Opener
Use the photo, the photo caption, and the questions on page 28 to get students to talk about the lesson topic. Begin a discussion about experiences in which the students gave messages that were understood by listeners. Ask questions such as:
- What kinds of words do you use when you give a positive message? A negative message?
- Is it possible to give a negative message without using harsh words?
- What can you do to look confident?

Follow Up—Extension Activity
Arrange to have magazines and newspapers for the activity. Choose pictures from the magazines and newspapers and ask students to imagine a message for each picture. Ask students to write a positive or negative message for each picture. Then discuss the messages with the class. Were any of the messages positive? Were any negative? Did the students' answers agree?

Portfolio Activity
Have students write a journal entry about a time they were confused by someone's message.

Lesson 5: Working with Different Styles (Pages 36–43)

Objectives
Students will learn:
- how to work with people who have different work styles.
- how to relate well with other people.

Vocabulary
aggressive, passive, assertive, interpersonal skills, point of view

Getting Started—Motivational Activity
Purpose: to demonstrate the importance of interacting well with others to complete common tasks.
1. Invite students to discuss any projects that they have accomplished with a group at school or at work.
2. Ask students to describe the leaders in their groups. Ask if there were any shy members in the groups.
3. Encourage students to conclude that every group is made up of the unique talents of each member. Point out that each member also has a unique working style.

Introducing the Lesson—Using the Unit Opener
Use the photo, the photo caption, and the questions on page 36 to get students to talk about the lesson topic. Begin a discussion about situations at school or work when you need to work with people who have different work styles to complete a task. Ask questions such as:
- What happens when one person takes charge of a group?
- How can you relate to and work well with other people?
- What do you do when someone disagrees with you?

Follow Up—Extension Activity
Ask the class to think of some examples of good interpersonal skills. Encourage students to think of words and phrases such as "Thank you" and "please." Also ask students to think of behaviors and actions that characterize good interpersonal relationships. For example, eye contact and listening skills encourage a speaker as he or she speaks. Have students think of ways that they like to be treated by coworkers, friends, and family members.

Portfolio Activity
Have students write a journal entry about a time they worked successfully in a group.

Communication

Lesson 6: Negotiating to Achieve Win-Win Solutions (Pages 44–51)

Objectives
Students will learn:
- how to work with people who have different points of view.
- how to relate well with other people.

Vocabulary
point of view, negotiation, compromise, creative problem solving, brainstorming

Getting Started—Motivational Activity
Purpose: to demonstrate that sharing ideas and different points of view can help groups meet goals.
1. Ask students to write a list of things that they hope to learn from this course.
2. Ask for a volunteer to read his or her list. Invite other students to read their lists.
3. Discuss anything that is common to the lists. Discuss any differences. Create a list of class goals. Post it in the room and review it periodically.

Introducing the Lesson—Using the Unit Opener
Use the photo, the photo caption, and the questions on page 44 to get students to talk about the lesson topic. Launch a discussion about how groups meet their goals. Think of school, home, or work groups. Ask questions such as:
- How do you decide what your goals are?
- How do you come up with new ideas as a group?

Follow Up—Extension Activity
Explain to students that sometimes a third party is necessary to serve as a mediator in a group to help facilitate the conversation. Ask students to work in groups of three. One person will defend the position that "it is better to work following high school than to go on to more schooling." The second person will defend the position that "it is better to go on to more schooling." The mediator should try to help the two other people defend their positions without using unnecessary or unpleasant behaviors or language. Help students conclude that people can defend different points of view without offending one another.

Portfolio Activity
Have students write a journal entry about a time they compromised to meet a group goal.

Lesson 7: Giving and Accepting Feedback (Pages 52–59)

Objectives
Students will learn:
- how to provide effective feedback.
- how to behave when accepting feedback.

Vocabulary
positive feedback, negative feedback, model

Getting Started—Motivational Activity
Purpose: to demonstrate that feedback is a two-way form of communication.
1. Ask students to work in groups of three. Have students write a list of characteristics of good relationships. Then ask them to write a list of things that can damage relationships (such as jealousy, gossip, criticism).
2. Invite one student to act out a good working relationship with you or another student. One person should act as a supervisor or boss. The other person should act as the employee or coworker.
3. Ask the class to conclude that good working relationships are based on good communication.

Introducing the Lesson—Using the Unit Opener
Use the photo, the photo caption, and the questions on page 52 to get students to talk about the lesson topic. Begin a discussion about how students learn from others at school, home, or work. Ask questions such as:
- How do you accept praise and compliments?
- How do you accept criticism?
- How do you compliment or correct someone else's behavior?

Follow Up—Extension Activity
Many people have trouble accepting and providing negative feedback. Explain to students that negative feedback is a helpful learning tool. Have students work with a partner. Ask groups to list ways to provide polite and helpful negative feedback. Students should also list appropriate ways to accept negative feedback. As a class, develop a list of guidelines for accepting and giving negative feedback. Encourage the class to follow these guidelines in the classroom.

Portfolio Activity
Have students write a journal entry about a time they received positive feedback.

Communication

Lesson 8: Performing in Today's Work Teams (Pages 60–67)

Objectives
Students will learn:
- how to be involved in a decision-making process.
- how to be a self-motivated member of a team.

Vocabulary
team, self-motivated, assign, analyze, create

Getting Started—Motivational Activity
Purpose: to demonstrate the responsibilities of being a member of a team.
1. Ask students to name some teams or work groups. Encourage students to list all kinds of teams—sports teams, emergency teams, home groups, or school groups. Record students' answers on a chalkboard. Then ask students to discuss the job titles of the people in these teams or groups. Write these on the board too. Help students to describe the roles of each person on the teams or groups.
2. Ask students what would happen if one or two people were left off the list. Could the team function if a member didn't come as expected? Why or why not? Encourage students to conclude that each member of a work team has responsibilities to the team.

Introducing the Lesson—Using the Unit Opener
Use the photo, the photo caption, and the questions on page 60 to get students to talk about the lesson topic. Begin a discussion about self-motivation and responsibility as a group member. Ask questions such as:
- What happens when one person in a group does all the work?
- How do you show that you are interested in your family's, class's, or coworker's goals?

Follow Up—Extension Activity
Ask students to think of a project for the class to do together. The project can be an improvement to the classroom, an outing or "field trip," or a study group. Have students decide how they will help their team or group. Encourage students to create a schedule, assign roles, and analyze methods for reaching their goal.

Portfolio Activity
Have students write a few sentences about specific ways they've contributed to a team.

Lesson 9: Communicating with Your Boss (Pages 68–75)

Objectives
Students will learn:
- how to be prepared for a supervisor's questions and requests.
- how to prepare well-written materials.
- how to speak clearly and concisely with a supervisor.

Vocabulary
legibly, oral report, anticipate, summary, concise

Getting Started—Motivational Activity
Purpose: to demonstrate that effective communication with a boss or supervisor is necessary.
1. Ask students to work with a partner. One person acts as the boss. The other person acts as an employee.
2. Have the bosses give instructions to copy and ship three packages to three people. The employees must memorize the instructions.
3. Have the workers repeat what the bosses said. Then discuss better ways to communicate the information. Would it be better to receive written instructions? Did the workers ask questions?

Introducing the Lesson—Using the Unit Opener
Use the photo, the photo caption, and the questions on page 68 to get students to talk about the lesson topic. Begin a discussion about why it's important to communicate well with a boss or supervisor. Ask questions such as:
- How do you rely on your teacher or boss?
- How does your teacher or boss rely on you?
- How do know when your teacher or boss is displeased with your performance?
- How do you know when your teacher or boss is pleased with your performance?

Follow Up—Extension Activity
Ask students to prepare written reports for the class. The reports should be one page—simple and concise. Students should report on a subject that they know about—a hobby, a sport, or other interest. Ask students to present their reports to the class.

Portfolio Activity
Have each student write a journal entry about a good relationship he or she has had with a teacher, mentor, or boss.

Communication

Lesson 10: Practicing Effective Telephone Communication (Pages 76-83)

Objectives
Students will learn:
- how to prepare for a call.
- how to speak and listen effectively to provide and take information.
- how to satisfy an angry caller.

Getting Started—Motivational Activity
Purpose: to demonstrate that effective telephone communication is necessary in business.
1. Have students imagine what would happen if the phone service was cut off for one day in a corporation. Ask students to think about what the communication would be like for the corporation's clients and suppliers.
2. Explain to students that ineffective telephone communication—disconnections, being on hold too long, rude behavior—within a business can have the same effect as having no service at all. Discuss the similarities between the two situations.

Introducing the Lesson—Using the Unit Opener
Use the photo, the photo caption, and the questions on page 76 to get students to talk about the lesson topic. Begin a discussion about telephone communication.
- How do you answer the phone on the job or at home?
- What information do you ask for if you want to give a message to another person?

Follow Up—Extension Activity
Ask students to work with a partner. One person acts as a worker receiving a call. The other person acts as an angry caller. Have students use the guidelines listed on page 77 to answer the call. Then ask them to refer to the guidelines on page 79 to satisfy the caller. Switch roles and repeat the activity.

Portfolio Activity
Have each student bring in a phone message they've taken or a message that was taken for them. Ask students to include the messages in their journals.

Time Management

Time Management

About the Book
Time-management skills are essential for survival in the workplace. Workers today need to develop the skills necessary to handle multiple tasks, establish priorities, and meet deadlines. By improving their time allocation and problem-solving skills, students will begin to see opportunities to work more efficiently and will feel a sense of satisfaction in accomplishing tasks on time.

This book covers such topics as setting goals and planning how to achieve them; adapting to changes in priorities; working with scheduling tools; managing crises; and identifying barriers to good time management.

Student Goals
- Develop skills for analyzing, prioritizing, and sequencing goals
- Understand how to be flexible and adjust to changes in resources, plans, and schedules
- Identify strategies useful for time management
- Learn how to identify and avoid situations that waste time

SCANS Foundation Skills

Workplace Competencies: Resources, Information, Interpersonal

Basic Skills: Reading, Listening

Thinking Skills: Decision Making, Problem Solving

Reading Skills: Understanding and Interpreting Written Information, Determining the Main Idea or Essential Message, Identifying Relevant Details

Time Management

Lesson 1: Setting Goals (Pages 4–11)

Objectives
Students will learn:
- how to identify goals.
- how to break down large tasks into smaller tasks.
- how to analyze, prioritize, sequence, and communicate goals.

Vocabulary
assignment, analyze, priorities, sequence

Getting Started—Motivational Activity
Purpose: to demonstrate that setting goals helps people accomplish tasks.
1. Ask volunteers to name some goals they meet each day. Examples might include completing a homework assignment or rearranging a shop's merchandise in time for a sale. Record the goals on the chalkboard.
2. Using the examples you recorded on the chalkboard, discuss why people set goals. How does setting goals provide a focus for what needs to be done? How does setting goals help work get done more efficiently?

Introducing the Lesson—Using the Unit Opener
Use the photo, the photo caption, and the questions on page 4 to get students to talk about the lesson topic. Start a discussion about times when students have goals for themselves in order to finish a task at school or work. Ask questions such as:
- What are some goals you have for this class?
- What steps can you take to achieve your goals?

Follow Up—Extension Activity
Have students work in groups to analyze the following assignment and set priorities: An owner of a new restaurant has the goal of opening her restaurant exactly one month from now. She has to finish the following tasks before the restaurant can open: hang pictures on the wall, get menus printed, hire waitstaff, train waitstaff, and place ads about the grand opening in the newspaper. Ask students to use the questions on page 6 to help them set priorities for the restaurant owner. Have volunteers from each group explain how their group decided on priorities.

Portfolio Activity
Have students write down a task they must complete within the next two weeks. Ask students to write a few sentences analyzing the task and stating how they will set priorities to complete the task.

Lesson 2: Planning (Pages 12–19)

Objectives
Students will learn:
- how to prepare in advance for a project.
- how to visualize a completed project.
- how to estimate the time a project will take.
- how to check on the progress of a project and communicate with coworkers about problems.
- how to make a schedule.
- how to review the results of a plan.

Vocabulary
false starts, materials, equipment, visualize, estimate, communicate, schedule

Getting Started—Motivational Activity
Purpose: to demonstrate that taking the time to plan something first saves time in the long run.
1. Discuss with students schedules they follow at work or school. Ask students to explain the purpose of these schedules. Discuss how the schedules help them complete tasks in a timely fashion.
2. Explain that a schedule is an important part of a plan. Schedules let people know about how long each part of a task will take. Schedules also help people keep track of their progress and how well their plan is working.

Introducing the Lesson—Using the Unit Opener
Use the photo, the photo caption, and the questions on page 12 to get students to talk about the lesson topic. Discuss with students the different kinds of plans they have made at school or work. Ask questions such as:
- How has planning saved you time?
- What problems can occur when you don't take time to plan?

Follow Up—Extension Activity
Have students think of a task they need to do in the next week or so. Have them estimate how long that task will take. Remind students to use any previous information they have about how long the task takes. Have students write down their estimate. Then ask them to keep track of the time the actual task takes. How close were their estimates? What could they do to improve their estimation skills?

Portfolio Activity
Have students write a journal entry in which they visualize the completion of an upcoming project at home, school, or work. They may include sketches of stages of the project if they wish.

Time Management

Lesson 3: Short-Term and Long-Term Planning (Pages 20–27)

Objectives
Students will learn:
- how to identify long- and short-term goals.
- how to gather information to help them plan.
- how to review the materials, equipment, and people needed to achieve a goal.
- how to make trade-offs to accommodate short- and long-term goals.

Vocabulary
long term, short term, resources, urgent, trade-off

Getting Started—Motivational Activity
Purpose: to demonstrate that short- and long-term planning are important aspects of time management.
1. Ask volunteers to explain their goals, or what they want to achieve, by taking this course. Explain that these goals are part of a long-term plan.
2. Then ask those volunteers how they plan to achieve these goals. Guide students in understanding that completing the lessons and the books of this course will help them work efficiently toward their long-term goal of completing the course.

Introducing the Lesson—Using the Unit Opener
Use the photo, the photo caption, and the questions on page 20 to get students to talk about the lesson topic. Discuss some examples of short- and long-term goals and the differences between the two types of goals. Ask questions such as:
- How does breaking a larger goal into smaller tasks help you stay on track?
- What process do you go through in deciding how to reach your goals?

Follow Up—Extension Activity
Have students work in small groups. Tell groups they are a team of recreation workers. Their long-term goal is to organize a fun fair day for children, which will take place in two months. Teams need to publicize the fair and organize events and activities for the children. Have groups make a list of some short-term goals that would help the team work toward their long-term goal.

Portfolio Activity
Ask students to write down one of their short-term goals and to make a list of the resources they need to accomplish that goal.

Lesson 4: Focusing (Pages 28–35)

Objectives
Students will learn:
- how to block out distractions while working.
- how to handle working with a talkative coworker.
- how to identify their most important tasks.
- how to keep track of time spent on a task.

Vocabulary
distractions, time sheet

Getting Started—Motivational Activity
Purpose: to demonstrate that the ability to focus results in being able to get more work done.
1. Ask volunteers to tell about a time at school or work when they were trying to get something done, but there was too much noise or too many outside interruptions. Ask students to include details of the reasons it was so hard to concentrate.
2. Have volunteers share their experiences with the class. Ask others to suggest what the person could have done to focus more fully on the task. Discuss with the class whether the suggestions would have helped get more work done.

Introducing the Lesson—Using the Unit Opener
Use the photo, the photo caption, and the questions on page 28 to get students to talk about the lesson topic. Launch a discussion about what it means to focus, or concentrate, on the work you are doing. Ask questions such as:
- What kinds of things distract you?
- How do distractions affect your work?

Follow Up—Extension Activity
Ask students to work in groups of three to role-play the following situation. Workers at a graphic design business work in open cubicles. Have two students act out the roles of Worker 1 and Worker 2, who work in cubicles next to each other. A third student should play Worker 3, who frequently meets with Worker 2 to discuss the project they are working on together. Sometimes they meet for half an hour. Worker 2 and Worker 3 talk very loudly during their meetings. Worker 1 finds this very distracting but doesn't know what to do since the conversations are about work. Have students role-play a way of dealing with the situation.

Portfolio Activity
Have students make a list of tips for staying focused and handling distractions.

Time Management

Lesson 5: Adjusting to a Change in Priorities (Pages 36–43)

Objectives
Students will learn:
- how to put priorities in order.
- how to find out deadlines and figure out how long a task will take.
- how to look at a task from an employer's point of view.
- how to be flexible and adjust to changes in resources, plans, and schedules.

Vocabulary
priority, resource, flexible

Getting Started—Motivational Activity
Purpose: to demonstrate that a change in priorities may make it necessary to change plans.
1. Ask volunteers to tell the class about their top priorities at work. Then ask volunteers to explain the kinds of things that can happen that cause their priorities to change. Have volunteers explain how they had to change their plans to adapt to the change in priorities.
2. Using the volunteers' examples, discuss with the class the kinds of skills that a worker must have to adapt to a change in priorities. Ask: How can a worker "switch gears" without losing a lot of time?

Introducing the Lesson—Using the Unit Opener
Use the photo, the photo caption, and the question on page 36 to get students to talk about the lesson topic. Start a discussion about times when a situation at work or school has caused priorities to change. Ask questions such as:
- How often did your priorities change in the past week?
- How did you react? What did you do?

Follow Up—Extension Activity
Have students work in groups to complete the Making Connections case studies on pages 41 and 42. Tell groups they have twenty minutes to complete the task. After ten minutes, change groups' priorities by telling them they must finish the task in fifteen minutes. After students have finished, discuss the methods students used to adapt to the unexpected change in deadline.

Portfolio Activity
Ask students to write a journal entry about why being flexible and able to adapt to changes at the workplace makes you a valued employee.

Lesson 6: Preventing Procrastination (Pages 44–51)

Objectives
Students will learn:
- how to avoid procrastinating.
- how to motivate themselves and maintain a positive attitude.
- how to mix work tasks.

Vocabulary
procrastination, motivation, self-starter

Getting Started—Motivational Activity
Purpose: to demonstrate that putting things off can cause serious problems for everyone involved.
1. Ask if any students know the meaning of the word *procrastination*. Help students understand that procrastination is delaying, or putting off, something that needs to be done.
2. Have several students volunteer some situations at home, school, or work in which they have procrastinated. Ask students to discuss why they procrastinated and what problems were caused by their procrastination. How did their procrastination affect others?

Introducing the Lesson—Using the Unit Opener
Use the photo, the photo caption, and the questions on page 44 to get students to talk about the lesson topic. Discuss with students some of the reasons people put off doing things. Ask questions such as:
- What kinds of tasks do you sometimes put off?
- How does putting off a task affect the quality of your work?

Follow Up—Extension Activity
Have students work in pairs. Ask students to interview two workers who have different types of jobs. One partner may interview one worker and the other partner can interview the other worker. Have students ask workers several questions about the methods they use to motivate themselves to do tasks they might otherwise put off. Have partners compare their findings and prepare a written report that discusses the workers' methods. Students should express an opinion about which methods would work best under different circumstances.

Portfolio Activity
Have students write down a task they often put off. Then ask them to list things they could do to motivate themselves to get the task done on time.

Time Management

Lesson 7: Keeping to Schedules (Pages 52–59)

Objectives
Students will learn:
- how to use tools such as a calendar, schedule, to-do list, routine, and tickler file to schedule time.
- how get information from references.

Vocabulary
calendar, deadline, to-do list, schedule, tickler file, reference, card file, routine

Getting Started—Motivational Activity
Purpose: to demonstrate that people are more productive if they keep to a schedule.
1. Have students name some of the schedules they follow in their personal life. (Students may name school or work schedules, bus or train schedules, and schedules for getting chores done at home.)
2. Discuss with students the benefits of keeping to a schedule. Ask: How does a schedule keep you from getting distracted? How do schedules help you keep track of your progress?

Introducing the Lesson—Using the Unit Opener
Use the photo, the photo caption, and the questions on page 52 to get students to talk about the lesson topic. Launch a discussion about times when students needed to stick to a schedule to accomplish something at work or school. Ask questions such as:
- When is it useful to make a schedule?
- How does a schedule help you accomplish tasks when you are working with a group or team?

Follow Up—Extension Activity
Review with students the purposes of calendars, tickler files, reference tools, and card files. Have students choose one of these tools to make. Ask students to use it at home or school. Several weeks later, invite volunteers to report to the class on how the tool has helped them keep to their schedules.

Portfolio Activity
Ask students to bring in a copy of a schedule or to-do list they have used.

Lesson 8: Managing Time During a Crisis (Pages 60–67)

Objectives
Students will learn:
- how to lower stress.
- how to gather information, list pros and cons, and rate decisions.
- how to arrange and group tasks.
- how to use downtime for short tasks.
- how to delegate work to coworkers.

Vocabulary
crisis, effective, downtime, delegating

Getting Started—Motivational Activity
Purpose: to demonstrate that good time management skills help people work through a crisis.

Tell the class that small and large crises happen while trying to do even routine tasks. Share a small crisis that you've dealt with recently and ask volunteers to share like experiences. Point out that time is very critical during a crisis and learning time-management skills can help them cope with last-minute changes.

Introducing the Lesson—Using the Unit Opener
Use the photo, the photo caption, and the questions on page 60 to get students to talk about the lesson topic. Ask students to discuss times they have had to deal with a crisis at school or work. Ask questions such as:
- What happens when you have too much work?
- What are some ways of handling stress at work?

Follow Up—Extension Activity
Handling stress is important during a crisis. Ask students to work in groups of four or five to brainstorm a list of ways to reduce stress. (Share one example with the class, such as taking a walk before or after work or school.)

Portfolio Activity
Have students write about someone who deals effectively with crises at work, school, or home.

Time Management

Lesson 9: Organizing Materials and Work Space (Pages 68–75)

Objectives
Students will learn:
- how to organize tools and materials.
- how to set up a filing system.
- how to respond to incoming documents.
- how to use technology as an organizing tool.
- how to customize shared work space.

Vocabulary
organized, efficiency, on-task, categories, filing system, in-box, database, customizing

Getting Started—Motivational Activity
Purpose: to demonstrate that keeping materials neatly organized saves time and helps you get work done.
1. Ask students if they have ever spent valuable time looking for an item on a messy desk or table. Ask volunteers to describe their feelings while trying to locate a "lost" item.
2. Point out that spending time looking for something is wasted time and can be avoided easily. Acknowledge that organizing your work spaces takes time but it can save your feeling panicked at the last minute when you can't find something you need.

Introducing the Lesson—Using the Unit Opener
Use the photo, the photo caption, and the questions on page 68 to get students to talk about the lesson topic. Ask students to discuss the disadvantages of a messy, disorganized work space. Ask questions such as:
- Do you think that keeping your work space neat can help you feel more in control of your work?
- What are some ways to keep an organized area neat?

Follow Up—Extension Activity
Have students arrange to visit a friend at his or her job. Ask students to take notes about the appearance of the person's work space. Have them consider the following questions: Are tools and materials easy to reach? Does the space look neat or messy? Does the person use computers or some other kind of technology? Have students give a brief oral report to the class describing the work space, summarizing its good points, and suggesting ways it could be better organized.

Portfolio Activity
Have students write a journal entry about how they might organize a work area at home, school, or work.

Lesson 10: Avoiding Time Wasters (Pages 76–83)

Objectives
Students will learn:
- how to think ahead.
- how to limit personal time at work and value other people's time.
- how to avoid getting "blocked."
- how to check their own progress.

Vocabulary
personal time

Getting Started—Motivational Activity
Purpose: to demonstrate that identifying time wasters can help people avoid them and get more work done.
1. Have the class brainstorm some examples from their own experiences of how time is sometimes wasted at the workplace. List students' examples on the chalkboard.
2. Invite students to think of some ways the situations listed on the chalkboard could be avoided or eliminated. Tell students that in this lesson they will learn how to recognize time wasters and how to avoid them.

Introducing the Lesson—Using the Unit Opener
Use the photo, the photo caption, and the questions on page 76 to get students to talk about the lesson topic. Launch a discussion about situations when students felt time was being wasted at school or work. Ask questions such as:
- Why do you sometimes feel that you can't get anything done?
- How can you avoid people or situations that unnecessarily take up a lot of your time?

Follow Up—Extension Activity
Have students keep a "time sheet" for one work day or school day. Ask students to write down all the tasks they do and the amount of time it took them to complete each task. Have students analyze their time sheets to find areas where they are not working as efficiently as they might. Have students put into practice some of the methods presented in the chapter. In several weeks, ask students to make another time sheet and evaluate their progress.

Portfolio Activity
Have students think of an upcoming project. Ask them to jot down some "planning ahead" ideas that will help them avoid situations that might result in wasted time.

Personal Development

About the Book

Most people would like to perform their job tasks well and progress in their careers. To be successful, employees need to know what their employers expect of them. Handling job responsibilities and exhibiting honesty and integrity are valuable characteristics that employers require and expect. To build a career and maintain job security, employees need to plan for success. Being a team player, monitoring performance, and facing fears and taking risks are parts of building a successful career.

This book covers such topics as meeting employer expectations; practicing self-assessment; accepting positive and negative feedback; building a support network; and accepting and handling responsibility.

Student Goals

• Understand their roles and responsibilities in the workplace
• Recognize the resources available for career advice and personal support
• Identify their values, strengths, and weaknesses
• Enhance their ability to manage stress, take risks, and overcome fears

SCANS Foundation Skills

Workplace Competencies: Interpersonal, Systems

Basic Skills: Listening, Speaking

Thinking Skills: Decision Making, Knowing How to Learn

Reading Skills: Looking for Details, Interpreting Written Information, Identifying Specifications

Lesson 1: Meeting Employer Expectations (Pages 4–11)

Objectives

Students will learn:
• how to show responsibility and demonstrate integrity and honesty.
• how to become self-motivated.
• how to practice self-management.

Vocabulary

responsible, integrity, self-motivated, self-management

Getting Started—Motivational Activity

Purpose: to demonstrate that employers expect their employees to be responsible, honest, and self-motivated.
1. Ask students to think of something they have accomplished that they are proud of, such as winning a basketball trophy or graduating from high school.
2. Discuss with students the methods they used to achieve their goal. Tell students that the ways they motivated, or drove, themselves to accomplish something important can and should be applied in the workplace. Self-motivation is one of the key skills employers look for. Explain to students that in this lesson they will learn how to use this skill at work.

Introducing the Lesson—Using the Unit Opener

Use the photo, the photo caption, and the questions on page 4 to get students to talk about the lesson topic. Discuss situations in which students have met with prospective employers. Ask questions such as:
• What questions can you ask in an interview to learn about an employer's expectations?
• How can you show an employer that you are responsible and honest?

Follow Up—Extension Activity

Have students work in pairs. Tell students to draft a list of questions an employer might ask a prospective employee about the person's honesty and integrity, sense of responsibility, and self-management skills. Students may want to invent hypothetical situations for some of their questions. Have students interview their partners. After the interview, the student acting as employer should write a statement explaining whether to hire the person. Partners should then switch roles.

Portfolio Activity

Have students list and describe in their journals three ways they show responsibility at home, work, or school.

Personal Development

Lesson 2: Practicing Self-Assessment (Pages 12–19)

Objectives
Students will learn:
- how to understand their assigned tasks.
- how to monitor and evaluate their job performance.
- how to create and complete a self-rating sheet.

Vocabulary
self-assessment, self-rating sheet

Getting Started—Motivational Activity
Purpose: to demonstrate that self-assessment can help improve job skills.
1. Discuss with students magazine quizzes that are designed to let people rate their exercise or nutrition habits or how well they manage money. If possible, bring a sample quiz to class. Ask students who have taken these quizzes if they were surprised at the results. Did they learn something about themselves? Did they try to change some of their habits as a result?
2. Tell students that such quizzes are a type of self-assessment. Explain that a self-rating sheet similar to the magazine quizzes is an excellent way to identify ways to improve job performance. Tell students that in this lesson they will learn about the steps involved in a job performance self-assessment.

Introducing the Lesson—Using the Unit Opener
Use the photo, the photo caption, and the questions on page 12 to get students to talk about the lesson topic. Ask students to think of times they have stepped back from something they were doing to check, or evaluate, their progress. Ask questions such as:
- How do you know you are performing a task well?
- How do you try to correct your performance?

Follow Up—Extension Activity
Ask students to write a job description for a job they do at home, school, or work for an "employee handbook." Students should describe all the tasks necessary to do the job. They may include advice about the job based on their own experiences. Students may also include rules or safety tips. After students have written their job descriptions, encourage them to think about how closely they follow their descriptions in actual practice.

Portfolio Activity
Have students write a journal entry in which they evaluate how well they do a daily task.

Lesson 3: Working with Others: Being a Team Player (Pages 20–27)

Objectives
Students will learn:
- how to take responsibility and follow through on personal and group goals.
- how to resolve group disagreements.
- how to show leadership.
- how to work as both a leader and a group member.

Vocabulary
teamwork, following through, resolving, leadership

Getting Started—Motivational Activity
Purpose: to demonstrate that effective teams are made up of individuals who follow through on their responsibilities.
1. Ask students to describe the work team that functions in an ordinary restaurant. Encourage students to list a waiter/waitress, host, cook, and so forth.
2. Invite three or four students to act out the roles of the restaurant staff for the class. You can act as the host, one student can act as a cook, and so forth.
3. Ask students what would happen if one of the team members did not follow through on his or her responsibilities. Help students conclude that the team would not succeed.

Introducing the Lesson—Using the Unit Opener
Use the photo, the photo caption, and the questions on page 20 to get students to talk about the lesson topic. Discuss with students how several different kinds of teams work together. Ask questions such as:
- What types of teams have you worked on at school or work?
- What talents and skills did members contribute?

Follow Up—Extension Activity
Have students work together in small groups to role-play a team of park workers who disagree about how to plant trees. Some workers think it would be better to dig all the holes first and then plant each tree. Others think it would be best to dig one hole and plant one tree before starting on the next tree. Remind students to listen carefully to the opinions of all team members and to keep an open mind as they work toward a resolution of the dispute. Have a member of each team describe for the class the skills their team used to solve the problem.

Portfolio Activity
Have students write a journal entry about a goal they accomplished through teamwork.

Personal Development

Lesson 4: Accepting Positive and Negative Feedback (Pages 28–35)

Objectives
Students will learn:
- how to listen constructively to feedback and use feedback to improve performance.
- how to stay calm while receiving feedback.
- how to thank people for positive feedback.
- how to analyze and discuss negative feedback.

Vocabulary
feedback, constructively

Getting Started—Motivational Activity
Purpose: to demonstrate that accepting feedback in an appropriate way can help improve job performance.

Ask students what they say when they receive a compliment. Do they say "thank you" or shrug it off due to embarrassment? Then explore how they feel when they hear negative feedback. Are they resentful or defensive or do they readily accept it? Explain that accepting positive and negative feedback is part of working. Students can learn how to handle feedback less emotionally so it helps them do better on the job.

Introducing the Lesson—Using the Unit Opener
Use the photo, the photo caption, and the questions on page 28 to get students to talk about the lesson topic. Begin a discussion about situations in which students received compliments or constructive criticism of their work. Ask questions such as:
- Why do people need to tell others they are doing something well?
- Why is it important to tell someone they are doing something incorrectly?

Follow Up—Extension Activity
Have students imagine a dialogue between an assistant manager and the manager of a health club. The manager has discovered that no one mopped the floors or arranged the equipment the night before when the assistant manager was in charge. Have pairs of students role-play a dialogue in which the manager gives the assistant manager negative feedback and the assistant manager does not listen constructively. Then have students revise the assistant manager's responses so that he or she accepts negative criticism constructively.

Portfolio Activity
Have students write some positive feedback about a task a coworker, family member, or classmate does well.

Lesson 5: Building a Positive Self-Image (Pages 36–43)

Objectives
Students will learn:
- how to identify their values and their strengths and weaknesses.
- how to project a positive self-image at work.
- how to bear in mind the reasons their job is important.

Vocabulary
self-image, values, interpersonal skills, technical skills

Getting Started—Motivational Activity
Purpose: to demonstrate that a positive self-image is a key to personal development in the workplace.
1. Read the following words aloud: *grouchy, moody, nervous, unsure.* Tell students these words might describe a worker with a negative self-image.
2. Then read the words: *cheerful, friendly, helpful, pleasant.* Tell students these words might describe a worker with a positive self-image.
3. Ask students which worker they would rather work with. Discuss with students which worker would get along better with coworkers, bosses, and customers.

Introducing the Lesson—Using the Unit Opener
Use the photo, the photo caption, and the questions on page 36 to get students to talk about the lesson topic. Discuss with students how people's feelings about themselves come across at the workplace. Ask questions such as:
- How does a confident person act or behave?
- Do you find it easier to deal with a confident or shy person? Why?

Follow Up—Extension Activity
Have students work in groups. Assign one of the jobs from the following list to each group: receptionist, flight attendant, car mechanic, paramedic, babysitter, firefighter, letter carrier, library worker, customer service representative, and bus driver. Ask groups to brainstorm a list of reasons why each job is important. Then have groups write a statement summarizing why people who do that job should take pride in their work. Invite groups to read their lists and statements to the class.

Portfolio Activity
Have students write a journal entry about one of their weaknesses and make a plan for overcoming that weakness.

Personal Development

Lesson 6: Building a Network (Pages 44–51)

Objectives
Students will learn:
- how to identify people who can offer career and job advice.
- how to build and maintain a network.

Vocabulary
network, maintain, role model, mentor, internal customers, external customers, emotional support

Getting Started—Motivational Activity
Purpose: to demonstrate how a network is useful as a career tool and as personal support.

Tell students that a network of people is like a tree of information. The people they know are like branches. Each friend, relative, or teacher knows many other people who may be a source of information to them. Encourage students to see that they probably have a network; they know many people working in different industries. Each person in their network could be a source of support and advice—maybe a job.

Introducing the Lesson—Using the Unit Opener
Use the photo, the photo caption, and the questions on page 44 to get students to talk about the lesson topic. Launch a discussion about how a network spans a person's entire personal and working life. Ask questions such as:
- Who are the people in your life who offer support and advice?
- Do you rely on certain people for information or other help in your career? What kinds of help do they give you?

Follow Up—Extension Activity
Have students write a list of people in their personal network—family members, friends, and neighbors. Ask students to write that person's job title—if applicable—next to each person's name. Help students identify the industry associated with each person on their individual lists. Then, as a class, list all of the different industries and varieties of jobs represented by the class list. Encourage students to think of this class list as another extension of their networks.

Portfolio Activity
Have students write a journal entry about a mentor, friend, or family member who has helped them in the past.

Lesson 7: Dealing with Stress (Pages 52–59)

Objectives
Students will learn:
- how to avoid certain types of stress.
- how to refocus energy to overcome negative stress.
- how to consider points of view and negotiate to control stress.
- how to maintain your health.

Vocabulary
stress, deadline, point of view, neutral, negotiate, compromise

Getting Started—Motivational Activity
Purpose: to demonstrate that everyone deals with stress and that it can be controlled.
1. Ask students to write a list of things that cause them stress. Have students divide their lists into two columns—everyday stress and long-term stress.
2. Collect the students' lists. Read the causes of stress, or stressors, to the class, but do not reveal the students' names.
3. Ask students to suggest ways to relieve stress. What are some ways that they try to relieve stress?

Introducing the Lesson—Using the Unit Opener
Use the photo, the photo caption, and the questions on page 52 to get students to talk about the lesson topic. Begin a discussion about causes of stress at work. Ask questions such as:
- Does stress serve any good purpose? Give an example.
- When can people be a source of stress?
- What kinds of situations are stressful to you?

Follow Up—Extension Activity
Ask students to name some jobs with high levels of stress—police officers, firefighters, emergency workers. Write the students' suggestions on the chalkboard. Have students think of sources of stress for these jobs and write them on the board. Based on the lesson, have students suggest ways of dealing with these sources of stress.

Portfolio Activity
Have students write a journal entry about how they deal successfully with everyday stress.

Personal Development

Lesson 8: Facing Fears and Taking Risks (Pages 60–67)

Objectives
Students will learn:
- how to resolve fears.
- how to avoid procrastination.
- how to take calculated risks and explore opportunities.

Vocabulary
warranted, procedures, procrastinate, risk, calculate

Getting Started—Motivational Activity
Purpose: to demonstrate that there are benefits to facing fears and taking risks.
1. On the chalkboard, list careers that regularly involve risks—such as emergency workers, electrical line workers, pilots.
2. List some of the risks associated with each career. Then ask students to think of some benefits of each career and list them on the board.
3. Encourage students to conclude that there are benefits to facing fears and taking risks.

Introducing the Lesson—Using the Unit Opener
Use the photo, the photo caption, and the questions on page 60 to get students to talk about the lesson topic. Begin a discussion about fears and risks in the workplace. Ask questions such as:
- What are examples of work situations that can be fearful?
- How do you know whether you should take a risk or not?

Follow Up—Extension Activity
Ask students to think of a situation when they were encouraged to do something they had never done before. Examples include attempting to participate in a new sport or going to an event such as a party where they did not know anyone else. Ask students to recall how the situation was presented to them. Ask students if they trusted the person who encouraged them. Have students write a paragraph about how the element of trust helped them make a decision to take the risk.

Portfolio Activity
Have each student write a journal entry about a risk they took and the benefit of that risk.

Lesson 9: Accepting and Handling Responsibility (Pages 68–75)

Objectives
Students will learn:
- why employers value people with a sense of responsibility.
- how to complete quality work.
- how to show respect to coworkers.

Vocabulary
sense of responsibility, consequences, punctual, feedback

Getting Started—Motivational Activity
Purpose: to demonstrate that having a sense of responsibility is necessary for getting and holding a job.
1. Ask students to make a list of their responsibilities—at work, home, and school.
2. Ask volunteers to describe how they feel when they do not meet a responsibility. How do they feel when someone doesn't meet a responsibility to them? Discuss these feelings as a class.
3. Tell students that employers expect a sense of responsibility from employees. Employers need to be able to depend on employees just as employees depend on employers.

Introducing the Lesson—Using the Unit Opener
Use the photo, the photo caption, and the questions on page 68 to get students to talk about the lesson topic. Begin a discussion about why a sense of responsibility is important for the workplace. Ask questions such as:
- How can one person's job affect another person's work?
- How can you show others that you care about your work?

Follow Up—Extension Activity
Ask students to use one sheet of paper to create life maps showing the responsibilities they have had and the responsibilities they see in the future. Ask students to write a list of their responsibilities chronologically. Then have students predict their responsibilities ten years in the future. Encourage students to include job, school, and family responsibilities. Help students conclude that accepting and handling responsibilities is about planning life goals.

Portfolio Activity
Have students write a journal entry about their most important responsibility.

Personal Development

Lesson 10: Preparing for Future Success (Pages 76–83)

Objectives
Students will learn:
- how to plan for a promotion.
- how to be valuable to employers.
- how to check on individual performance.

Vocabulary
promotable, monitor, asset, verbal, performance appraisal

Getting Started—Motivational Activity
Purpose: to demonstrate that making a plan and following through are necessary steps for getting a promotion.
1. Ask students to list one goal they would like to accomplish this week or month—fix the car, make an improvement to the home, or complete a school assignment.
2. Have students list a target date for the goal and an expected benefit of their goal.
3. Ask students if there are any steps they need to take to meet that goal. Do they need to accomplish part of the goal each week? Do they need to earn money to meet the goal? Do they need training?

Introducing the Lesson—Using the Unit Opener
Use the photo, the photo caption, and the questions on page 76 to get students to talk about the lesson topic. Launch a discussion about how a promotion is the result of effort and planning.
- What are some ways that employers reward employees?
- On what basis should promotions be given?

Follow Up—Extension Activity
Have students work with a partner. Ask groups to select one career they would like to know more about. Have students visit a library, career resource center, or school to learn more about that career. Or students might interview someone in that career. Have students prepare a short report listing the steps of how to reach that career goal—including a timetable of the career path. Ask groups to present their findings to the class.

Portfolio Activity
Have students collect information to put in their portfolio about a career that they are interested in.

Customer Service

Customer Service

About the Book
In many companies today, customer service is no longer the exclusive province of a few representatives. Rather, these companies are emphasizing that all their employees are engaged in customer service. The emphasis is on all employees—as individuals, as part of teams, and as part of their company overall—taking responsibility to meet customers' needs.

This book covers such topics as identifying internal and external customers and learning their needs; communicating clearly and accepting feedback; working as part of a team; resolving problems with dissatisfied customers; using technology to provide good customer service; taking initiative; and cultivating positive relations with customers.

Student Goals
- Identify internal and external customers and understand their needs
- Understand the importance of good listening, clear speaking, and concise writing
- Appreciate the benefits and requirements of customer service teams
- Know how to deal with dissatisfied customers
- Understand the uses of technology in developing customer service
- Know how to cultivate all-around good customer service relationships

SCANS Foundation Skills

Workplace Competencies: Information, Interpersonal, Technology

Basic Skills: Listening, Speaking

Thinking Skills: Decision Making, Problem Solving, Knowing How to Learn

Reading Skills: Identifying Facts, Making Judgments

Customer Service

Lesson 1: Who Are Your Customers? (Pages 4–11)

Objectives
Students will learn:
- how to identify internal and external customers.
- how to appreciate the importance of good customer service.

Vocabulary
external customers, clients, internal customers

Getting Started—Motivational Activity
Purpose: to demonstrate the importance of providing good customer service.
1. Have the students organize into pairs for a role play. In each pair, one student will be a customer and the other will represent a company from which the customer has bought a product or a service.
2. Tell the customer in each pair to approach the company representative with a complaint. Tell the company representative to try to respond so as to satisfy the customer.
3. Then have the students switch roles. Have the company representative give a response that is not helpful.
4. Conclude by asking students to remark on the ways they were treated in their roles as customers.

Introducing the Lesson—Using the Unit Opener
Use the photo, the photo caption, and the questions on page 4 to get students to talk about the lesson topic. Have students discuss situations at school or work when they were not happy with a product, service, or information they received. Ask questions such as:
- Did they know whom to approach to raise a question, complaint, or criticism?
- Did they feel comfortable raising their concerns?
- Were they satisfied with the response that they got?

Follow Up—Extension Activity
Ask students to work in groups of three. Provide groups with a list of stores providing products to a specific group of customers—a local sporting goods store, a clothing store, a food market. Have groups brainstorm a list of customers for each store. Encourage students to identify the sex, age, and interests of the customers. As a class, discuss the group lists. Write students' customer lists on the board. Ask students what criteria they used to identify the customers of the stores.

Portfolio Activity
Have students write a journal entry about a time when they had to deal with a complaint from a customer.

Lesson 2: Identifying Your Customers' Needs (Pages 12–19)

Objectives
Students will learn:
- how to listen carefully by keeping an open mind, keeping quiet, and avoiding distraction.
- how to speak clearly to be understood, including by repeating customers' messages in the students' own words.

Vocabulary
proactive listener, reflection, body language

Getting Started—Motivational Activity
Purpose: to demonstrate how speaking and listening carefully are vital to providing good customer service.
1. Divide students into groups of five or six. Tell one student in each group the same brief message.
2. Instruct these students to tell the person to their right this message—word for word. (They should whisper in each other's ears so no one else hears.)
3. Ask the last person to hear the message from each group to share the message with the class.

Introducing the Lesson—Using the Unit Opener
Use the photo, the photo caption, and the questions on page 12 to get students to talk about the lesson topic. Encourage students to discuss situations when they felt that others were not paying attention to what they were saying. Ask questions such as:
- How could they tell the other person was not paying attention?
- How did being ignored make them feel?
- Did they do or say anything to express how they felt?

Follow Up—Extension Activity
For class discussion, bring in a customer service survey from a store or restaurant. Explain the survey and read the questions to the students. Discuss the information that the organization is trying to collect. Ask students how the information can improve the organization's efforts to provide good customer service. Ask students to think of other questions that might be included on the survey.

Portfolio Activity
Have students write a journal entry about a time when someone misunderstood what they had said.

Customer Service

Lesson 3: Representing Your Company (Pages 20–27)

Objectives
Students will learn:
- how to know their company's goals and structure.
- how to understand their company's competition and the industry as a whole.

Vocabulary
represent, industry, mission statement, competition

Getting Started—Motivational Activity
Purpose: to show the importance of employees understanding their company's goals.
1. Ask students to think about previous and current employers they have had. Help students to recognize the industry and goods and services of each business. Then help students to list the main goals of these companies. Write the company goals on the board.
2. Discuss any similarities among the goals. Then ask students to list ways that the employees help to meet the company's main goals. Help students conclude that employees must understand the goals of the company they work for.

Introducing the Lesson—Using the Unit Opener
Use the photo, the photo caption, and the questions on page 20 to get students to talk about the lesson topic. Have students offer ideas about the importance of knowing their company's goals. Ask questions such as:
- Is it enough to carry out your own task and not think about how it fits into the company's work overall?
- Why do customers assume that employees' attitudes are the same as those of the company?

Follow Up—Extension Activity
Create a list of companies that work regularly with the public, such as shipping, mailing, and delivery service companies; utility companies; transportation companies. Write the names of the companies on the board. Ask students to describe the appearance of the company employees who work in the field. What kind of clothing do they wear? Why do you think appearance is important? How is their appearance a reflection of their company?

Portfolio Activity
In their journals, have students write a few sentences explaining their company's or school's goals.

Lesson 4: Being Part of a Customer Service Team (Pages 28–35)

Objectives
Students will learn about:
- the benefits of working on a customer service team.
- giving and accepting feedback.
- being a productive team member.
- developing teamwork and responsibility.

Vocabulary
follow through, feedback

Getting Started—Motivational Activity
Purpose: to show that working well as part of a team means doing more than simply bringing people together.
1. Ask students to think about movies, music videos, TV programs, plays, or sports events. Ask volunteers to give examples of talented actors, musicians, or athletes that they saw perform as part of a group or team.
2. Do they think these individuals worked well as part of their casts, bands, or teams? Why or why not? What makes a team successful? Help students conclude that every individual needs to contribute to a team effort.

Introducing the Lesson—Using the Unit Opener
Use the photo, the photo caption, and the questions on page 28 to get students to talk about the lesson topic. Have students brainstorm about the advantages of working in teams.
- Give an example of a task that lends itself to teamwork, such as building a house. Ask students to come up with other examples.
- Give an example of a work process where some things are best done in teams (such as work in a restaurant) and other tasks that are best done individually (such as work by a hair stylist or dentist). Ask students to offer explanations of why they think this is so.

Follow Up—Extension Activity
Involve students in a discussion of the meaning of the phrase, "the whole is greater than the sum of the parts." Point out that teamwork does not mean an end to individual responsibility; rather, it puts individuals' contributions in a different context.

Portfolio Activity
Have students write a journal entry that gives an example of feedback they've given or accepted as part of a team at school, work, or home.

Customer Service

Lesson 5: Dealing with Dissatisfied Customers (Pages 36–43)

Objectives
Students will learn:
- why customers may become dissatisfied.
- what methods they can use to resolve a conflict with a dissatisfied customer.

Vocabulary
proactive

Getting Started—Motivational Activity
Purpose: to illustrate how good customer service can be used with customers who are angry.
1. Ask a few volunteers to role-play different situations before the class. Organize them into pairs.
2. In each pair, have one student be a dissatisfied customer, and the other be a service representative. The customer should have a legitimate grievance, but brings it up in an angry or rude way.
3. The service representative should try to act calmly and attentively to resolve the situation to the customer's satisfaction.
4. Encourage students to conclude that there are effective ways to deal with dissatisfied customers.

Introducing the Lesson—Using the Unit Opener
Use the photo, the photo caption, and the questions on page 36 to get students to talk about the lesson topic. Ask students to recall situations when they were the "angry customer." Examples include waiting to purchase tickets or a product and then finding out that the item is no longer available. Ask questions such as:
- Did they get angry with the ticket agent or the sales clerk? Did they think first about whether these people were really responsible for the problem?
- How did the customer service people in these situations respond? Were the customers satisfied?

Follow Up—Extension Activity
Point out to students that many situations with dissatisfied customers can be defused "on the spot," but the problems may need further attention. Guide them to talk about how good customer service often means doing follow-up. Ask students to work in groups of three. Have them construct a list of steps for a typical customer complaint requiring follow-up. Help students by listing the first two steps: taking the customer request and investigating the customer's original purchase.

Portfolio Activity
Ask students to write a journal entry about a time when their request for customer service was followed up.

Lesson 6: Using Telephone Skills with Customers (Pages 44–51)

Objectives
Students will learn:
- how to answer the phone at work.
- how to put the customer at ease over the phone.
- how to use their best voice when on the phone.

Vocabulary
pitch, tone

Getting Started—Motivational Activity
Purpose: to demonstrate the importance of using one's "best" voice when talking on the phone.
1. Ask students to recall experiences when they could not understand someone on the phone. Encourage students to think of calls from a business or other organization. Invite volunteers to describe their experiences to the class.
2. For each experience, invite students to analyze the points of confusion. Did the person speak too quickly? Too softly? Write students' suggestions on the board.
3. Help students to conclude that employees need to speak clearly, at a reasonable pace and volume, to communicate well with customers.

Introducing the Lesson—Using the Unit Opener
Use the photo, the photo caption, and the questions on page 44 to get students to talk about the lesson topic. Launch a discussion about why customer service representatives must make it clear to every customer who calls them that the company is giving his or her request its total attention. Ask questions such as:
- How can a worker who may receive dozens of phone calls every day from customers make each one feel that his or her request is important?
- What will happen if the company representative sounds bored or tired over the phone?

Follow Up—Extension Activity
Explain to the class that many large companies have installed automatic telephone-answering equipment. Typically it directs callers to choose different options on push-button phones. Ask students to discuss their experiences with this kind of equipment. What do they think are its advantages or disadvantages? What happens if customers can't get answers by choosing any of the available options?

Portfolio Activity
Have students keep a log of calls made and received and note the purpose and outcome of each call.

Customer Service

Lesson 7: Developing Positive Relationships with Customers (Pages 52–59)

Objectives
Students will learn:
- how to greet and welcome customers.
- how to show courtesy, enthusiasm, and respect.
- how to establish trust.
- how to help customers get information.

Vocabulary
courteous, enthusiasm

Getting Started—Motivational Activity
Purpose: to explore the difference between a sincere commitment to customer service and an insincere "hustle" or "hype."
1. Ask students to work with a partner. Have students discuss good customer service experiences and poor customer service experiences.
2. Ask them to create two lists. The first list should include characteristics of the good service they received. The second list should include characteristics of the poor service they received.
3. Ask volunteers to read their lists and write them on the board. Help students conclude that good customer service is based on trust.

Introducing the Lesson—Using the Unit Opener
Use the photo, the photo caption, and the questions on page 52 to get students to talk about the lesson topic. Encourage students to talk about building trust with customers. Ask questions such as:
- How do you feel when a store clerk or other worker follows through on your request?
- What do you think when a worker pays more attention to a phone call than to your request for assistance?

Follow Up—Extension Activity
Ask students to work in groups of four. Have them brainstorm a list of workers that often establish positive, lasting relationships with customers. Dentists, doctors, hair stylists, and food service workers are examples. Ask students why they think these are often long-lasting relationships. Why are they unique? Help students conclude that customers usually buy services from people they trust.

Portfolio Activity
Have students write a journal entry about someone they know who has extended excellent customer service to them.

Lesson 8: Writing Letters (Pages 60–67)

Objectives
Students will learn:
- how to use a "customer-friendly" tone in writing business letters to customers.
- how to communicate necessary information.
- how to write concisely.

Vocabulary
formal tone, informal tone, concise, wordiness

Getting Started—Motivational Activity
Purpose: to demonstrate the importance of writing in a friendly or polite manner.
1. Prepare two or more business letters. Highlight parts of the letter that use friendly or polite language.
2. Present the letters to the class. Explain the purpose of each letter. Then, read the highlighted parts. Ask students to describe those parts. What words were used to make the letter friendly? Are the letters trying to persuade the recipient to do something?
3. Help students conclude that people are more likely to read and respond to letters that are written in a polite or friendly way.

Introducing the Lesson—Using the Unit Opener
Use the photo, the photo caption, and the questions on page 60 to get students to talk about the lesson topic. Encourage them to discuss what a business letter can accomplish that conversation on the phone or in person cannot. Ask questions such as:
- Why is it important to have a permanent record of a conversation or an understanding between a company and a customer?
- Are there times when a business letter can succeed in getting information from a customer or another company but a phone conversation cannot? Why?

Follow Up—Extension Activity
Tell students that there may be situations when they should get information in writing—when they buy a new product or service, when they need price information. Explain to students that in some cases a contract is required. Ask students to work in groups of three. Have groups brainstorm to create a list of business transactions that are best to have in writing. Encourage students to think of important transactions, such as an apartment or auto lease, or a home mortgage.

Portfolio Activity
Have students write a journal entry about a business letter they received. Was it clear or confusing? Why?

Customer Service

Lesson 9: Using Technology (Pages 68–75)

Objectives
Students will learn:
- how to use technology to give better customer service.
- how to find out about using available technology.
- how to understand basic technologies.
- how to use basic computer software functions.

Vocabulary
technology, copier, fax, facsimile machine, voicemail system, modem, database, spreadsheets, computer network, e-mail, word processing, mail merge, backup files, Internet, download

Getting Started—Motivational Activity
Purpose: to illustrate some of the ways that technology has improved the workplace since the 1950s.
1. Ask the class to imagine that they are working in an office 40 years ago. They need to send a one-page business letter to 50 different companies. The tools available are a manual typewriter, pens and pencils, erasers, and carbon paper (explain).
2. Ask students several questions about this project. How would the letter get produced? How would copies be made? How would errors be corrected? What if parts of the letter had to be changed?
3. Ask students to guess how much time would have been needed for one person to complete this project.

Introducing the Lesson—Using the Unit Opener
Use the photo, the photo caption, and the questions on page 68 to get students to talk about the lesson topic. Involve students in a discussion about changes resulting from technology in the workplace. Ask questions such as:
- What are some examples of new kinds of technology that have changed the workplace?
- How have the kinds of work that people do changed as a result of computers? What kinds take less time?
- How have these changes affected people's ability to provide good customer service?

Follow Up—Extension Activity
Ask students to suggest ways that they can learn more about new technology in their community. Guide the discussion to include information about college courses, resources in the public library, educational TV programs, and information on the Internet.

Portfolio Activity
Ask students to write a journal entry about their reactions when they first encountered a computer.

Lesson 10: A Commitment to Superior Service (Pages 76–83)

Objectives
Students will learn:
- how to demonstrate loyalty to customers.
- how to ask for input from customers.
- how to monitor their behavior with customers.
- why to provide superior customer service.

Vocabulary
superior, competitive edge, loyalty, innovative, monitor

Getting Started—Motivational Activity
Purpose: to convey a sense of what it means to provide superior service.
1. Ask students to write a list of things they do well. Encourage students to think of small and large tasks—maintaining a car, creating a particular meal, following a budget, taking photographs.
2. Then ask students to write a sentence or two that explains why they are good at this particular task.
3. Collect student lists and read some examples. Do not reveal the identity of the writer. Help students conclude that in each case the individual did something extra—put forth his or her best effort.

Introducing the Lesson—Using the Unit Opener
Use the photo, the photo caption, and the questions on page 76 to get students to talk about the lesson topic. Briefly explain to students the meaning of *innovation*. Encourage them to talk about the qualities of an innovative person. Ask questions such as:
- Does the innovative employee rely on "tried and true" solutions?
- What does an innovator do if he or she is given instructions that do not make sense?
- How can people's ability to innovate be further developed?

Follow Up—Extension Activity
Bring in magazines and newspapers containing articles about individuals and businesses that have provided superior customer service. Read one of the articles. Ask students to work in groups of three. Help students identify the strengths of the person or the company. Ask groups to choose a group leader to describe to the class what gives the company or person a "competitive edge."

Portfolio Activity
Ask students to write a journal entry about a way they have been innovative while working on a project at work, at school, or at home.

Problem Solving

Problem Solving

About the Book
Problem-solving skills are vital for the workplace environment. Employers in manufacturing- and service-oriented businesses rely on employees' ability to solve problems. In many workplaces, employees are expected to solve problems independent of management and often within a work team. Workers must have the logical, cognitive thinking skills to carry out a problem-solving process to meet work goals.

This book covers such topics as identifying a problem; finding causes of a problem; creating a plan and putting it into action; reviewing and revising solutions; applying problem-solving skills as a team; and using technology to solve problems.

Student Goals
- Develop skills for recognizing problems; gathering and interpreting information; and identifying causes and devising solutions
- Understand why plans need to be reviewed and revised; understand how technology can help solve problems
- Enhance self-confidence in meeting challenges; enhance interpersonal skills for working with groups

SCANS Foundation Skills

Workplace Competencies: Interpersonal, Information, Resources, Systems, Technology

Basic Skills: Reading, Writing, Listening, Speaking

Thinking Skills: Decision Making, Problem Solving

Reading Skills: Understanding Written Information, Interpreting Written Information, Determining the Main Idea, Identifying Relevant Details, Inferring the Meaning of Unknown or Technical Vocabulary

Lesson 1: Identifying Problems (Pages 4–11)

Objectives
Students will learn:
- how to identify problems.
- how to gather, organize, and interpret information.
- how to use problem-solving strategies.

Vocabulary
identify, problem, categories

Getting Started—Motivational Activity
Purpose: to show how to gather information as a necessary step in solving a problem.
1. Have students work in groups of four. Ask groups to brainstorm a list of common problems with completing work or school tasks—not enough time, too much to do, difficult subject matter. Have students discuss whether they think the problems are easy to solve.
2. Explain to students that this book will show them strategies for solving problems in the workplace. A series of steps will be presented to help find solutions.

Introducing the Lesson—Using the Unit Opener
Use the photo, the photo caption, and the questions on page 4 to get students to talk about the lesson topic. Involve students in a discussion about what it means to identify a problem. For example, suggest a scenario in which employees are trying to meet a weekly production quota but discover they are falling behind. Ask questions such as:
- How do the employees know that a problem exists?
- What would happen if they did not realize there was a problem?

Follow Up—Extension Activity
Ask students to work in groups of four. As a class, brainstorm a list of places in the community—supermarkets, public transportation facilities, restaurants, check-cashing services. Assign each group a place. Have each group create a list of problems that the workers in its place might have to solve. Discuss the problems as a class.

Portfolio Activity
Have students write a journal entry about a time when they did not realize they had a problem of some kind at work or at school, and someone else identified it.

Problem Solving

Lesson 2: Finding Causes of Problems (Pages 12–19)

Objectives
Students will learn:
- how to create a list of possible causes.
- how to research possible causes by observing and asking questions.
- how to analyze causes.

Vocabulary
analyze, observing

Getting Started—Motivational Activity
Purpose: to show some of the ways of investigating possible causes of a problem.
1. Invite students to talk about their favorite mystery or detective TV shows. Help them create a list of methods that investigators use to identify the perpetrators of crimes. Write this list on the board.
2. Help the class group these methods into broad categories, such as: considering all the possible suspects; observing and interviewing them; gathering information about them from other sources; and analyzing the data. Help students conclude that these are ways of investigating the cause of a problem. Ask the students whether searching for the cause of a problem is like being a detective.

Introducing the Lesson—Using the Unit Opener
Use the photo, the photo caption, and the questions on page 12 to get students to talk about the lesson topic. Launch a discussion of what it means to analyze a problem. Ask questions such as:
- How do you manage complicated problems? Do you ask people to help you?
- How can it help to break a problem down into smaller parts?
- Is discovering the cause of a problem the same as solving it? Why or why not?

Follow Up—Extension Activity
Bring in an article from a current magazine or newspaper that presents a local problem, such as parking, unemployment, pollution, etc. Summarize the article for the class. Ask the class to identify the problem. List on the chalkboard the causes mentioned in the article or brainstorm a list of causes. Ask the class for some suggestions for solving the problem.

Portfolio Activity
Have students write a journal entry about how they found the cause of a problem at work, school, or home.

Lesson 3: Creating a Solution (Pages 20–27)

Objectives
Students will learn:
- how to determine elements for reaching a solution.
- how to create possible solutions.
- how to predict results.
- how to weigh advantages and disadvantages.

Vocabulary
compromise, needs, wants, predict, advantages, disadvantages

Getting Started—Motivational Activity
Purpose: to illustrate the process of a group reaching a compromise.
1. Ask four volunteers to role-play a situation in which they are trying to decide how to spend a free evening together on a weekend.
2. Each person has a strong preference for how to spend the evening, such as going to a movie, going bowling, playing cards at someone's home, or taking a walk. (The volunteers may wish to supply other ideas.)
3. Instruct the volunteers to work out their differences and arrive at a plan for what they want to do together. Conclude the activity by reviewing the steps they went through to reach a decision.

Introducing the Lesson—Using the Unit Opener
Use the photo, the photo caption, and the questions on page 20 to get students to discuss the lesson topic. Ask students to talk about what it means to make a prediction. Ask questions such as:
- Have you ever based a solution on experience? Describe such a situation.
- Do you generally rely on old solutions to problems, or do you try to create new solutions to problems?

Follow Up—Extension Activity
Have students work in groups of three. Lead a discussion about the pros and cons of buying a new or a used car. Then ask groups to predict the outcomes of choosing one of these options. Ask each group to make a decision to buy either a new or a used car. As a class, discuss how the groups weighed the advantages and disadvantages of each option—and ultimately came to their decision.

Portfolio Activity
Have students write a journal entry about a time when they had to reach a compromise with someone else.

Problem Solving

Lesson 4: Making a Plan and Putting It into Action (Pages 28–35)

Objectives
Students will learn:
- how to create a plan of action.
- how to delegate responsibility.
- how to distinguish high- and low-priority tasks.

Vocabulary
solution, plan of action, delegate, high-priority tasks, low-priority tasks

Getting Started—Motivational Activity
Purpose: to illustrate what it means to put things in order of priority.
1. Ask students to think of plans that they have helped put into action. Examples may include organizing a sports team or planning a special ceremony.
2. Have students write a list of steps they used to contribute to that plan. Did they attend practices as part of a team? Did they make a list of party supplies for a birthday celebration?
3. Explain to students that these are examples of making a plan and putting it into action. Ask students if the plans helped them reach their goals.

Introducing the Lesson—Using the Unit Opener
Use the photo, the photo caption, and the questions on page 28 to get students to talk about the lesson topic. Lead a discussion about how to decide whether you need a plan to solve a problem. Use a scenario such as the following: A neighborhood association wants to raise money to buy backboards and baskets for a local playground. Ask questions such as:
- Is this problem simple or complex?
- Are there many people involved in the solution to this problem? (Include who would make requests for funds and who would make donations.)
- Is a plan needed to raise this money? Why?

Follow Up—Extension Activity
Ask each student to write a list of everything that needs to be done that day. Ask volunteers to describe ways that they try to plan each day—by breaking tasks into morning, afternoon, or evening; by grouping similar tasks. Ask students if some tasks are more important than others. Do they do those tasks first? Ask students to explain their answers.

Portfolio Activity
Have students write a journal entry about a time when they created an action plan at work or at school.

Lesson 5: Reviewing and Revising Plans (Pages 36–43)

Objectives
Students will learn:
- how to monitor a plan.
- how to figure out why a plan isn't working.
- how to revise a plan.
- how to create a backup plan.

Vocabulary
monitor, revise, backup plan

Getting Started—Motivational Activity
Purpose: to show the importance of monitoring a plan.
1. Draw a simple picture of a one-mile racetrack on the chalkboard. Ask students to suppose that they are running in a one-mile race. Their plan is to run at a comfortable pace for three-quarters of a mile (point out where this is on your drawing), then speed up during the last quarter-mile.
2. When they reach the half-mile point (point out), they decide they will fall too far behind the leaders if they wait until the last quarter to speed up.
3. What are their options at the half-mile point? Do they need to revise their plan? Help students to state other times they might have to revise a plan.

Introducing the Lesson—Using the Unit Opener
Use the photo, the photo caption, and the questions on page 36 to get students to talk about the lesson topic. Discuss why it's not enough just to make a plan. Rather, every plan should be tested in practice and periodically reviewed. Ask questions such as:
- Does having a plan mean you will achieve your goal?
- If your plan doesn't work, does that mean you should throw it out and start over? Why or why not?
- Is it wise to have a second, or backup, plan in reserve? Why or why not?

Follow Up—Extension Activity
Explain how to develop *criteria* to decide if a plan works. Have students write the following questions on a sheet of paper: Did the plan solve the problem? Did any part of the plan not work? Did the plan create additional work or costs? Did the plan create a new problem? Was the plan easy to put into action? Invite students to add other questions to this list. Then ask volunteers to tell about a plan they used—answering each of the questions.

Portfolio Activity
Have students write a journal entry about a time when their plan did not work out and they had to change it.

Problem Solving

Lesson 6: Working as a Team (Pages 44–51)

Objectives
Students will learn:
- how to assess problems to decide on a problem-solving approach.
- how to choose the best group problem-solving method.
- how to brainstorm to create ideas.
- how to use the private participation method.
- how to make both authority- and group-based decisions.

Vocabulary
assess, brainstorming, private participation, authority, authority-based decision, group-based decisions, consensus

Getting Started—Motivational Activity
Purpose: to demonstrate that some problems are better solved by a work team than by an individual.
1. Have students work in small groups. Ask students to write a catchy slogan for a refreshing sports drink called Chill Factor. They should emphasize the drink's benefits for people who train seriously for competitive sports. Give groups 5 to 10 minutes to work on a slogan.
2. Have each group read its slogan. Discuss the processes that groups used to create their slogan. Did group members decide together or did one or two people make the decisions? Which way is better?

Introducing the Lesson—Using the Unit Opener
Use the photo, the photo caption, and the questions on page 44 to get students to talk about the lesson topic. Discuss with students why problems are sometimes better solved by a group. Ask questions such as:
- How do you know when a problem is too big for you to solve alone?
- Who do you ask to help you?
- What advice or assistance can these people offer that you do not have?

Follow Up—Extension Activity
Ask students to work in groups of three. Assign the brainstorming, private participation, or authority-based decision method to each group. Give each group a production schedule or staff problem to solve using their assigned method. Discuss group solutions and processes for reaching the solutions.

Portfolio Activity
Have students write a journal entry about a time when they worked with a group to solve a problem.

Lesson 7: Meeting New Challenges (Pages 52–59)

Objectives
Students will learn:
- how to be flexible in responding to challenges.
- how to view challenges in a positive way.
- how to use problem-solving skills to meet challenges.

Vocabulary
challenge, temporary, permanent

Getting Started—Motivational Activity
Purpose: to demonstrate that problem-solving skills help people meet challenges in the workplace.
1. Explain what new challenges mean in the lesson context. (A new challenge is a change that poses difficulties.)
2. Have students name some new challenges they have encountered in the month. Discuss ways they could use the material in Lessons 1–6 to help deal with these challenges.
3. Have students write one way that they can use the information in previous lessons to meet one of their new challenges.

Introducing the Lesson—Using the Unit Opener
Use the photo, the photo caption, and the questions on page 52 to get students to talk about the lesson topic. Launch a discussion about difficult tasks students have had to deal with. Ask questions such as:
- Do people ever find change frightening? Why or why not?
- Is change good or bad? What can you do to make change easier?

Follow Up—Extension Activity
Have students work with a partner to role-play a situation in which a supervisor tells a worker that he or she will have to take on the duties of another employee while that employee is on vacation. Students may draw from their own experiences in creating the scenario. Remind students to demonstrate a positive attitude in meeting the temporary challenge.

Portfolio Activity
Have students write a journal entry in which they describe a possible temporary challenge that could occur at school, work, or home and explain how they would meet that challenge.

Problem Solving

Lesson 8: Keeping Up with Technology (Pages 60–67)

Objectives
Students will learn:
- how to keep up with new technology and view it in a positive way.
- how to find out about resources to learn more about technology.

Vocabulary
technology, manual, spreadsheet

Getting Started—Motivational Activity
Purpose: to demonstrate that keeping up with changing technology is very important in today's workplace.
1. Challenge students to think of new kinds of office technology that have appeared in the last 10 to 15 years (personal computers, voice mail, fax machines, cellular phones). Discuss some of the changes these types of technology have brought about for workers.
2. For each of the types of technology mentioned, discuss its advantages. Ask students who have used the technology to share their experiences learning how to use it. Did they at first feel frightened or threatened by it? How did they feel after they learned how to use it?

Introducing the Lesson—Using the Unit Opener
Use the photo, the photo caption, and the questions on page 60 to get students to talk about the lesson topic. Discuss with students the kinds of technology they use at home, work, or school. Ask questions such as:
- What types of technology do you currently use? How did you learn to use it?
- How can technology help you do your job better?

Follow Up—Extension Activity
Have students discuss ways they can use technology to complete more work or to do better work. Begin by listing on the board examples of technology in the workplace: calculators, computers, photocopiers, specific software applications. Ask students to contribute ideas to the list. Have students choose the technology from the list that would help them. Ask volunteers to tell how the technology would be useful.

Portfolio Activity
Have students write a journal entry about a type of technology they would like to learn to use and how they would go about learning it.

Lesson 9: Getting Along with Others (Pages 68–75)

Objectives
Students will learn:
- how to maintain polite, friendly behavior.
- how to understand cultural differences and put themselves in other people's shoes.
- how to get along with their boss.

Vocabulary
assertive

Getting Started—Motivational Activity
Purpose: to illustrate the importance of being able to "put yourself in someone else's shoes."
1. Describe the following workplace situation to students. Tamara asks Joanne for help with a project. Joanne says that she will help as soon as time is available. Later, Joanne always seems to be busy.
2. Ask the class to offer ideas for how Tamara should respond in this situation. Does Tamara appreciate that Joanne is very busy with other work? Does Joanne understand that Tamara places importance on the project she has asked Joanne to help with?
3. Help students conclude that understanding others' priorities and points of view prevents misunderstandings and feelings of resentment.

Introducing the Lesson—Using the Unit Opener
Use the photo, the photo caption, and the questions on page 68 to get students to talk about the lesson topic. Have students discuss why it is important to get along well with others on the job. Ask questions such as:
- If you have the technical skills your work requires, do you still have to get along with others?
- Does getting along with others only affect your work—or does it affect others' work as well?

Follow Up—Extension Activity
Define the following terms: *assertive* (polite, firm, self-confident) and *passive* (shy, withdrawn). Have students work in groups of three. Assign one of the terms to each group and have groups create conversations in that style. Ask groups to present their conversations to the class. The rest of the class should figure out the type of conversation acted out by the group. How might the passive people become more assertive?

Portfolio Activity
Ask students to write a journal entry about a time when they were not getting along well with someone, but eventually they were able to work things out with the other person.

Problem Solving

Lesson 10: Managing Stress (Pages 76–83)

Objectives
Students will learn:
- how to take care of their physical health and use physical activity to manage stress.
- how to eliminate or control situations that cause stress.
- how to talk about stress.
- how to modify their goals to reduce stress.

Vocabulary
stress, positive stress, negative stress, eliminate, modify

Getting Started—Motivational Activity
Purpose: to demonstrate the benefits of learning how to manage stress.
1. Tell students that several kinds of illnesses are caused by repeated exposure to stress. Stress resulting from rapid technological changes, inflation, changing roles in the workplace, constant decision making, and many other factors can cause ulcers, headaches, heart disease, anxiety, high blood pressure, and other disorders.
2. Ask volunteers to name some sources of stress in their lives or the lives of people they know. Then tell students that many strategies have been developed for managing stress and that in this lesson they will learn how to use some of these strategies.

Introducing the Lesson—Using the Unit Opener
Use the photo, the photo caption, and the questions on page 76 to get students to talk about the lesson topic. Launch a discussion about what it means to be "stressed out." Ask questions such as:
- How do you feel when you are under stress?
- How do you help others who are under stress? What advice do you provide?

Follow Up—Extension Activity
Hold a class discussion about the negative ways people deal with stress (lashing out at others, skipping meals, smoking, watching too much TV, and so on). Record students' responses on the board. Discuss why these negative strategies do not address the causes of stress and do not provide a satisfactory solution to managing stress. Then have them list some more positive ways to deal with stress, such as getting more exercise.

Portfolio Activity
Have each student make a personal top-ten list of "stress busters." Encourage students to refer to their list during stressful times.

Writing

Writing

About the Book
Basic writing skills are a necessary component of conducting business and personal dealings. Businesses report that the ability to write is a crucial skill that is often not found in new hires. People entering the workforce need to develop their basic writing skills to improve their employment opportunities and personal interactions.

To facilitate the development of students' writing skills, this book covers a variety of business documents, including resumes, cover letters, memos, e-mail, and reports. A writing Handbook is at the end of the book and provides information on spelling, grammar, punctuation, and other rules of the English language. The Handbook also presents a simplified form of the writing process steps.

Student Goals
- Develop skills for writing to organize information and prepare for a job
- Develop writing skills that are basic for every workplace
- Understand what employers expect from applicants and employees

SCANS Foundation Skills

Workplace Competencies: Information, Systems, Technology

Basic Skills: Reading, Writing

Thinking Skill: Decision Making

Reading Skills: Understanding Written Information, Interpreting Written Information, Determining the Main Idea, Identifying Relevant Details

Writing

Lesson 1: Personal Data Sheet (Pages 5–6)

Objectives
Students will learn:
- the uses of a personal data sheet.
- how to create a personal data sheet.

Getting Started—Motivational Activity
Purpose: to show how a personal data sheet can be a valuable tool as students begin to look for work.
1. Bring in some sample job listings and give one to each pair of students. Ask pairs to participate in a role play. One will act as a personnel officer at a company listed in one of the ads. The other will be a job applicant calling to ask about the job opening.
2. The personnel officer will ask: What kind of job experience do you have? What skills do you have? Have students ask more job-related questions.
3. Ask students how the caller might prepare for this call. Reinforce the concept that the caller needs to create a written record of experiences and skills to answer questions quickly and to be well-organized.

Introducing the Lesson—Using the Unit Opener
Use the sample personal data sheet in the lesson to get students to talk about the lesson topic. Involve students in a discussion about why certain kinds of information should be included on a personal data sheet. Ask questions such as:
- Why is it important to list the name, address, and phone number of each previous employer?
- Why is it important to describe the kind of work you did and what kind of training you received?
- Why should you contact people first and get their permission if you want to list them as references?

Follow Up—Extension Activity
Engage the students in more discussion about the differences between specific job experiences and skills. For example, they may have experience taking care of animals, but this experience does not reflect the writing or math skills that they learned in school. Remind students that it is important to include both kinds of information on a personal data sheet because potential future employers may not be familiar with particular tasks.

Portfolio Activity
Ask students to make a journal entry listing people who might be good personal references.

Lesson 2: Application Form (Pages 7–11)

Objectives
Students will learn:
- how to fill out a job application.
- why application forms are important.

Getting Started—Motivational Activity
Purpose: to illustrate the correct way to fill out an application.
1. Ask students to relate what kinds of experience they have had with filling out forms. Encourage students to think of insurance forms, rental agreements, and bank forms.
2. Ask them why a job application form is important in possibly getting a new job.

Introducing the Lesson—Using the Unit Opener
Use the sample application form in the lesson to get students to talk about the lesson topic. Launch a discussion about why it is important to fill out an application form completely, honestly, and accurately. Ask questions such as:
- Why is it important to be as accurate as possible when filling out an application?
- How does an employer use the application form?

Follow Up—Extension Activity
Define the word *credit* for students as the right to buy something now and pay for it later. Discuss bank and store credit cards with students. Have students work in groups of three. Explain that a bank or store takes a financial risk by giving an applicant credit. Then, have groups create a list of responsibilities as a credit card holder. Have each group share its list with the class.

Portfolio Activity
Ask students to make a journal entry about the first time they applied for a job, credit card, or recreation pass.

Writing

Lesson 3: Resume (Pages 12–14)

Objectives
Students will learn:
- the function of a resume.
- how to create a resume.

Vocabulary
resume, outline, format, references

Getting Started—Motivational Activity
Purpose: to illustrate the use of a resume.
1. Ask students to think about this situation. An employer has put a notice in the newspaper advertising a job opening. The employer gets fifty calls from people who are interested in the job. However, the employer only has time to interview five people.
2. Ask the class how the employer can decide who to interview from the group of fifty people. Lead them to conclude that the employer can quickly skim over the resumes to select the top five.

Introducing the Lesson—Using the Unit Opener
Use the sample resume in the lesson to get students to talk about the lesson topic. You may want to make it into a transparency. To get the discussion going, ask questions such as:
- What do employers use resumes for?
- What is the usual format of a resume?
- What kinds of information are necessary? What kinds are optional? What kinds of questions should not be asked?

Follow Up—Extension Activity
Explain to students that resumes are like sales tools. Strong, carefully prepared resumes highlight the specific talents and skills of the individual. Which skills to emphasize may vary depending on which job the person is applying for. Have students work in groups of three. Ask groups to create a fictional resume for someone who would like to be a restaurant manager. Help groups think of job and school skills and experiences to create the resume. Remind students to try to "sell" the individual's talents and skills. Have groups share their fictional resumes with the class.

Portfolio Activity
Ask students to write a journal entry about the number one selling point that they would include about themselves on a resume.

Lesson 4: Cover Letter and Business Envelope (Pages 15–18)

Objectives
Students will learn:
- the uses of a cover letter.
- how to compose a cover letter.

Vocabulary
formal

Getting Started—Motivational Activity
Purpose: to illustrate the uses of cover letters.
1. Tell students that a resume is a standard document with which most employers are familiar. A resume is a factual piece of information about an individual. A cover letter accompanies a resume and may point out unique features about the prospective employee. Ask students what the correct tone for a cover letter is—a formal tone.
2. Ask them whether cover letters should be long and thorough, or short and concise.
3. Ask what they think may happen to resumes that are sent to employers without cover letters.

Introducing the Lesson—Using the Unit Opener
Use the sample cover letter in the lesson to get students to talk about the lesson topic. Encourage students to participate. Ask questions such as:
- What might happen to a resume if the envelope is poorly prepared?
- Companies receive many resumes, often for many different job openings. How would you know how to organize these resumes and route them to the appropriate managers if you worked in a company's personnel department?
- Can cover letters eliminate potential confusion?

Follow Up—Extension Activity
Have students imagine that they are sending their resumes to many employers. Ask them how they could have some specific content in the information they provide to each particular employer, without having to redo their resume each time. Guide the students to the conclusion that "customized" cover letters that address specific points in particular job listings are a good solution.

Portfolio Activity
Ask students to bring in examples of envelopes they have received and include them in their journals. Have students label the different parts of the envelope.

Writing

Lesson 5: Follow-Up Letter (Pages 19–21)

Objectives
Students will learn:
- the uses of a follow-up letter.
- how to write a follow-up letter.

Vocabulary
follow-up letter, proofread

Getting Started—Motivational Activity
Purpose: to illustrate the importance of a follow-up letter.
1. Explain to students that the interviewing process is often a time-consuming task for an employer.
2. Tell students that they should express gratitude for the interviewer's time and attention; this can be expressed in person at the end of the interview. A follow-up letter also serves this purpose.
3. Ask students what other thoughts they might express in a follow-up letter. Help them conclude that this letter makes the applicant stand out from other applicants.

Introducing the Lesson—Using the Unit Opener
Use the sample follow-up letter in the lesson to get students to talk about the lesson topic. Ask questions such as:
- Is it required for all job applicants to write a follow-up letter to the company?
- How can a follow-up letter give a sense of the applicant's enthusiasm?
- What can a follow-up letter show the company about the applicant?

Follow Up—Extension Activity
Point out that as a general rule, even though they receive large quantities of mail, employers like to receive follow-up letters because in this way they learn more about the applicants. Ask students what the employer might think if a follow-up letter included a misspelled word. Discuss how important it is to pay attention to details of the letter.

Portfolio Activity
Have students bring in thank-you notes they have received or other documents that expressed thanks. Have them include their documents in their journals.

Lesson 6: Forms: W-4, I-9, and Medical Insurance (Pages 22–28)

Objectives
Students will learn:
- three forms employers require of new employees.
- how to fill out those forms.

Vocabulary
income, withhold

Getting Started—Motivational Activity
Purpose: to illustrate what is involved in filling out medical insurance forms.
1. Ask students, by a show of hands, to indicate how many of them have a written record of their medical history at home.
2. Ask students where they can get information about their medical history. Help students to conclude that doctors, dentists, and family members are sources of this information.

Introducing the Lesson—Using the Unit Opener
Tell students that they will see examples of kinds of writing that they are likely to do on a job. This lesson focuses on forms. Use the sample forms in the lesson to get students to talk about the lesson topic. Explain that employers and state and federal government agencies require information about every worker. Ask questions such as:
- What experience do you have in filling out income tax forms?
- What are some examples of personal information documents?

Follow Up—Extension Activity
Tell students that medical insurance is a benefit supplied by an employer. Medical insurance is expensive and some businesses—particularly small ones—cannot afford to offer this benefit to employees. Ask students to work in groups of three. Have groups create a list of other benefits offered by employers. Ask each group to share its list with the class.

Portfolio Activity
Have students write an entry in their journal about any previous job they had or their parents had and whether it provided medical insurance to the employee.

Lesson 7: Writing with a Computer (Pages 29–32)

Objectives
Students will learn about:
- some applications of computers in writing.
- basic and more advanced computer functions.

Vocabulary
word processor, input, select, edit, delete, save, backing up, undo, search/find/replace

Getting Started—Motivational Activity
Purpose: to show the importance of acquiring computer skills.
1. Bring in the classified ads. Choose different categories of job listings and pass them out to the students.
2. Ask students to circle all the ads that require computer skills. Ask them to write a question mark next to ones about which they are not sure.
3. Tabulate the results on the chalkboard and discuss the results with the class. Calculate for them what percentage of the jobs that are open in particular fields require computer skills.

Introducing the Lesson—Using the Unit Opener
To get students talking about the lesson topic, ask questions such as:
- What are examples of different ways that businesses are using computers?
- Why is it important to acquire computer skills to prepare for the workplace?
- Do you use a computer?

Follow Up—Extension Activity
Bring in a catalog selling software. Explain the various applications—to design documents such as brochures, books, newsletters; to illustrate; to manipulate photos; to edit video programs. Encourage students to think of ideas for software—to create financial information—or to volunteer to discuss different software that they have seen or used. Refer to the catalog to see if the students' software ideas or products are in the catalog.

Portfolio Activity
Have students bring in a computer-generated document such as a letter, receipt, or bill. Have them include it in their journals.

Lesson 8: Memos (Pages 33–35)

Objectives
Students will learn:
- when memos are appropriate.
- how to write memos.

Vocabulary
internal communication, policy

Getting Started—Motivational Activity
Purpose: to illustrate the function of memos in the workplace.
1. Ask students to think of situations in which information was provided to them within a group. Encourage students to think of class, family, or community groups.
2. Ask students to discuss situations in which information was provided in writing. Did they receive a letter, a short note, or a flyer?
3. Help students understand the function of a memo in the workplace—it communicates brief information to a group of people.

Introducing the Lesson—Using the Unit Opener
Use the sample memo in the lesson to get students to talk about the lesson topic. Discuss the meaning of the word *memo*—short for *memorandum*—which means an informal record or reminder. Ask questions such as:
- What purpose can a memo serve that a phone call cannot serve?
- When would a memo be appropriate?

Follow Up—Extension Activity
Ask each student to write a short memo to the class. The memo should contain one idea for how to improve the class sessions. Ask volunteers to read their memos to the entire class.

Portfolio Activity
Have students write a journal entry about a time when they were not aware of an important policy at school or at work. Ask them to tell whether they think a memo would have helped get the message out.

Writing

Lesson 9: E-Mail and Phone Messages (Pages 36–39)

Objectives
Students will learn:
- the uses of e-mail and phone messages.
- the kinds of information that should be included in e-mail and phone messages.

Vocabulary
reply

Getting Started—Motivational Activity
Purpose: to demonstrate different means of communicating messages.
1. Ask students to think of the people that they communicate with regularly by phone. Have them include friends, coworkers, family members, supervisors, or customers.
2. Ask students what happens when they miss a call from one of these people. Is a message provided to them? Have they ever received an incomplete message?
3. Ask students if they know what e-mail is. Explain e-mail and how it is similar to communicating by phone or phone messages.

Introducing the Lesson—Using the Unit Opener
Use the sample phone and e-mail messages in the lesson to get students to talk about the lesson topic. Ask questions such as:
- What kind of information should you get from a caller if you are taking a message for someone else?
- Why is it a good idea to write a message rather than just rely on your memory?

Follow Up—Extension Activity
Have students interview someone they know who works for a company that uses e-mail on a regular basis. They should ask what kinds of messages are transmitted in this way, how long it usually takes to get responses, and in what situations the company prefers to send memos, regular mail, or other means of communication.

Portfolio Activity
Have students write a journal entry about what they say when they answer the telephone at home and take a message for someone else.

Lesson 10: Performance Appraisal (Pages 40–44)

Objectives
Students will learn:
- the purpose of a performance appraisal.
- how to prepare for a performance appraisal.

Vocabulary
rate, confidential

Getting Started—Motivational Activity
Purpose: to demonstrate the interaction during a performance appraisal.
1. Ask two volunteers to role-play. One student will be the supervisor during a performance appraisal, and the other will be the employee.
2. Ask the class to suggest ideas for what kind of work skills the supervisor should evaluate. Also ask them to suggest ideas for how the employee should respond.
3. Have the volunteers enact the performance appraisal. Ask the class whether the employee will get a good rating.

Introducing the Lesson—Using the Unit Opener
Use the sample performance appraisal in the lesson to get students to talk about the lesson topic. Ask questions such as:
- What is the purpose of a performance appraisal?
- What kinds of things are evaluated in a performance appraisal?
- Who would use the information on an appraisal?

Follow Up—Extension Activity
Point out to students that although many businesses conduct regular performance appraisals of all employees, others do not. Ask students to brainstorm ideas about what they should do if they were to work in a company where they had not received an appraisal for well over one year.

Portfolio Activity
Have students write a journal entry that lists three strengths noted in a performance appraisal they received at school or work.

Writing

Lesson 11: Form Letters (Pages 45–48)

Objectives
Students will learn:
- how to use a database file and a word processing file.
- how to merge the two files.
- how to work efficiently when creating many similar letters.

Vocabulary
merge, database, fields, boilerplate

Getting Started—Motivational Activity
Purpose: to demonstrate the structure of a form letter.
1. Make photocopies of two form letters and bring them to class.
2. Ask students to study the form letters. Have students note any similarities between the two letters.
3. Explain the purpose of a form letter. Help students conclude that form letters contain some generic information and usually some information particular to the individual.

Introducing the Lesson—Using the Unit Opener
Ask students to refer to the sample form letter and database file in the text to talk about the lesson topic. Begin a discussion about the purpose of form letters. Ask questions such as:
- Can you think of an example of when you might need to write the same letter to several people?
- Which parts of a form letter stay the same?
- Which parts of a form letter change from letter to letter?

Follow Up—Extension Activity
Bring in examples of form letters and invite students to do the same. As a class, analyze the different parts of the letters. Ask them to identify the header and boilerplate information on each letter. Which information is different from letter to letter? Which is the same? How are they signed?

Portfolio Activity
Have students write a journal entry about a form letter they received that was especially pleasing or displeasing.

Lesson 12: Customer Service Letters (Pages 49–51)

Objectives
Students will learn:
- how to request information and action from customers.
- how to respond to customer inquiries.
- how to provide information for customers.

Vocabulary
order

Getting Started—Motivational Activity
Purpose: to demonstrate that some forms of communication should be in writing.
1. Show students some examples of communication that are best given in writing—bills, bank account statements, and contracts.
2. Ask students why it is best to have these forms of communication in writing. What facts or details should be presented in writing? Why might you need proof that you paid a bill or made a bank deposit?

Introducing the Lesson—Using the Unit Opener
Refer students to the sample customer service letter on page 50. To introduce it, ask volunteers to identify the five different parts of a business letter: heading, inside address, greeting, body, and closing. Ask further questions such as:
- What company sent this letter?
- To whom is this letter addressed?
- What might this letter be about?

Follow Up—Extension Activity
Have students work in groups of three. Ask the groups to think of a product or service that they would like to know more about. Ask each group to write one business letter requesting some information about the product or service and trade letters with another group. Have groups write a business letter in response. Ask groups to share their letters with the class.

Portfolio Activity
Have students write a journal entry about why a customer service letter should have a polite tone.

Writing

Lesson 13: Reports (Pages 52–55)

Objectives
Students will learn:
- about different types of reports.
- how to collect information for reports.
- how to structure a report.

Vocabulary
research, topic, progress report, recommend, survey, sequence, chronological, conclusion

Getting Started—Motivational Activity
Purpose: to demonstrate that writing a report is similar to a memo, which students know how to write.
1. Review the purpose of a memo from Lesson 8. Focus students' attention on the following: to request action, to summarize, or to update.
2. Encourage students to think of a report as a long memo. Ask students for examples of situations in which a memo would not provide enough information. If they cannot think of any, tell them that detailed financial information for projects involving large sums of money is often presented in the form of reports.

Introducing the Lesson—Using the Unit Opener
Refer to the sample report on page 54 to get students to talk about the lesson topic. Begin a discussion about situations at school or work when reports are required. Ask questions such as:
- What is the purpose of a report?
- How do you collect information for a report?

Follow Up—Extension Activity
Ask students to work in groups of three. Provide students with a list of topics about companies that would interest them. Companies might include an entertainment company, a local business, or an international corporation. Topics might include a new product or service, a contribution to the community, or an interesting fact about another culture. Have each group prepare a one-page report about one of the topics. Encourage groups to visit a library and collect information. Ask groups to share their reports with the class.

Portfolio Activity
Have students write a journal entry about a report they have written or read in the past.

Handbook (Pages 56–82)

Designed as a supplement to the 13 lessons in the *Writing* book, this Handbook provides written instruction and practice of the grammar, spelling, and punctuation skills basic to success in the workplace. In addition, it presents the four stages of the writing process (gathering and organizing ideas, writing, checking, and revising). The Handbook can be used in a variety of ways:

For independent use: As learners work through the first part of the *Writing* book, note any errors individuals make in mechanics, usage, and structure, and assign learners to the appropriate pages in the Handbook.

For whole-class instruction: You can have the class work through the sections on mechanics, usage, and structure in any order you wish. First go over a section with learners. Then assign the instruction and exercises for learners to read and complete as homework or in class.

For teaching the writing process: Students can work through the instruction on the writing process at any point in the lessons. We recommend presenting the writing process prior to or concurrently with the first three lessons in the book. To present each stage of the writing process, present the material in the book to learners. Then have learners read the instruction independently and complete the exercises as homework or in class.

You can check students' work, or they can correct their own work, using the Answer Key on pages 89–92. If you wish, you can remove the entire Answer Key from students' books. If you notice that learners are having trouble completing the exercises correctly, you may want to assign them to Steck-Vaughn's *Language Exercises for Adults, Skills for Success: Writing,* or other appropriate materials before having them continue with this Handbook or the lessons in this book.

Workforce: Building Success
Certificate of Completion

This is to certify that

_____

*has successfully completed the Communication book
of the Steck-Vaughn Workforce: Building Success series.*

STECK-VAUGHN
COMPANY
ELEMENTARY • SECONDARY • ADULT • LIBRARY

The Leader in Adult Education

_____
Instructor

_____
Organization or Program

_____
City and State   *Date*

Workforce: Building Success

Certificate of Completion

This is to certify that

_____

has successfully completed the Time Management book of the Steck-Vaughn Workforce: Building Success series.

_____
Instructor

_____
Organization or Program

_____
City and State   *Date*

STECK-VAUGHN
C O M P A N Y
ELEMENTARY • SECONDARY • ADULT • LIBRARY

The Leader in Adult Education

Workforce: Building Success
Certificate of Completion

This is to certify that

has successfully completed the Personal Development book
of the Steck-Vaughn Workforce: Building Success series.

Instructor

Organization or Program

City and State   _Date_

STECK-VAUGHN
C O M P A N Y
ELEMENTARY • SECONDARY • ADULT • LIBRARY

The Leader in Adult Education

Workforce: Building Success
Certificate of Completion

This is to certify that

_____

has successfully completed the Customer Service book of the Steck-Vaughn Workforce: Building Success series.

_____
Instructor

_____
Organization or Program

_____
City and State   Date

STECK-VAUGHN
C O M P A N Y
ELEMENTARY • SECONDARY • ADULT • LIBRARY

The Leader in Adult Education

Workforce: Building Success
Certificate of Completion

This is to certify that

_____

has successfully completed the Problem Solving book
of the Steck-Vaughn Workforce: Building Success series.

_____
Instructor

_____
Organization or Program

_____
City and State   Date

STECK-VAUGHN
C O M P A N Y
ELEMENTARY • SECONDARY • ADULT • LIBRARY

The Leader in Adult Education

Workforce: Building Success
Certificate of Completion

This is to certify that

_____

has successfully completed the Writing book
of the Steck-Vaughn Workforce: Building Success series.

_____
Instructor

_____
Organization or Program

_____
City and State

_____
Date

STECK-VAUGHN
COMPANY
ELEMENTARY • SECONDARY • ADULT • LIBRARY

The Leader in Adult Education